Overcoming Disparity

Latino Young Men and Boys

Profiles in Best Practice

Edited by Frank de Jesús Acosta
and Henry A. J. Ramos

Arte Público Press
Houston, Texas

Overcoming Disparity: Latino Young Men and Boys is funded in part by grants from California Community Foundation, the California Endowment, Marguerite Casey Foundation, City of Houston through the Houston Arts Alliance, W. K. Kellogg Foundation and Sierra Health Foundation. We are grateful for their support.

Recovering the past, creating the future

Arte Público Press
University of Houston
4902 Gulf Fwy, Bldg 19, Rm 100
Houston, Texas 77204-2004

Cover design by Mora Des¡gn
Cover art, "Semilla," by Alicia Maria Siu

Names: Jesús Acosta, Frank de, editor. I Ramos, Henry A. J., 1959— editor.
Title: Overcoming disparity : Latino young men and boys / Frank de Jesús Acosta, editor; Henry A. J. Ramos, coeditor.
Description: Houston, TX: Arte Publico Press, 2016.
  Identifiers: LCCN 2015050505I ISBN 9781558858305 (trade pbk.) I ISBN 9781518500923 (Kindle) I ISBN 9781518500930 (pdf)
  Subjects: LCSH: Hispanic American young men—Social conditions. I Hispanic American young men—Services for. I Poor youth—United States—Services for. I Juvenile delinquency—United States—Prevention. I Equality—United States.
Classification: LCC HV3187.A2 O94 2016 I DDC 362.84/68073—dc23
LC record available at http://lccn.loc.gov/2015050505

16 17 18 19 20   7 6 5 4 3 2 1

Table of Contents

Acknowledgments

All honor to our ancestors. We thank our philanthropic partners, the California Endowment, W. K. Kellogg Foundation, Sierra Health Foundation, Marguerite Casey Foundation and California Community Foundation, without whose support we could not have completed this project.

Tlazocamati ("thank you" in the Nahuatl language of our forebears) to all of the Latino men and boys (and women) who contributed art, poetry and writings or otherwise supported the hard work that it took to complete this ambitious endeavor.

Our organizational partners (particularly the leadership, staff, volunteers and participants of Communities United for Restorative Youth Justice, Barrios Unidos, Homies Unidos, Homeboy Industries, La Plazita and In-and-Out Writers) graciously took time from their vital daily work and responsibilities to help make this work's completion a community-wide effort. We are forever indebted to these leaders for their inspiration and their valued collaboration, both of which speak volumes about their undying commitment to and love of humanity.

We are also fundamentally grateful to the youth, men, advocates and leaders (especially our incarcerated brothers) who gave of their hearts, considerable gifts, wisdom and time in support of our efforts throughout the completion of this volume and the larger series of examinations of which it is a part.

Last but not least, we are eternally beholden to our illustrious Project Advisory Group, whose dedication and support in connection with this work was essential to its completion. Following are the members of this impressive collection of leading national experts and practitioners on the issues:

Luis Rodríguez
Tía Chucha's Centro Cultural
Sylmar, CA

Albino García, Jr.
La Plazita Institute
Albuquerque, NM

Daniel "Nane" Alejandrez
Barrios Unidos
Santa Cruz, CA

Jerry Tello
National Compadres Network
Whittier, CA

George Galvis
Communities United for Restorative Youth Justice
Oakland, CA

Rubén Lizardo
University of California
Berkeley, CA

Alex Sánchez
Homies Unidos
Los Angeles, CA

Javier Stauring
Healing Justice Coalition
Los Angeles, CA

Father Greg Boyle, SJ
Homeboy Industries
Los Angeles, CA

Richard Montoya
Culture Clash
Los Angeles, CA

Carmen Pérez
The Gathering for Justice
New York, NY

Tomás Alejo
Washington, DC

Luis Cardona
Baltimore, MD

Patrick Mulcahey
Whittier, CA

In Lak'ech Hala Ken (Mayan saying: "I am the other you, and you are the other me").

Editors' Note

Frank de Jesús Acosta and Henry A. J. Ramos

Overcoming Disparity: Latino Young Men and Boys provides surveys about the leading programs and strategies that effectively engage young Latino men and boys in ways that expand their prospects for crafting healthy, productive, prosperous and socially contributing lives. It builds on two prior publications that we have produced on the issues in recent years: *The History of Barrios Unidos: Healing Community Violence* (Arte Público Press, 2007), by Frank de Jesús Acosta, which features the work of Barrios Unidos (one of the nation's most evolved networks working with at-risk Latino men and boys through cultural awareness, community service and healing interventions); and *Latino Young Men and Boys in Search of Justice: Testimonies* (Arte Público Press, 2016), edited by Frank de Jesús Acosta and Henry A. J. Ramos, highlighting the creative voice of California Latino men and boys (many of whom are currently or were formerly incarcerated) in the form of original poetry, essays, drawings, paintings, tattoo art and murals.

In publicizing the experiences and perspectives of young Latino males and those who work most effectively on their behalf relative to community organizing and the economy, violence prevention and justice, health and education, and culture and art, our goal is, in large part, to humanize these young men on the public stage. Too frequently, mainstream media and leaders have demonized Latino men and boys along with African American and other minority males, generally perceiving and representing them as criminals, predators, drug traffickers or general drags on our economy and civic culture. In fact, there are many data and much evidence to explain the perception of Latino men and boys by outside observers as a troublesome population subgroup. Recent government and scholarly data reveal that Latino men and boys are among the nation's most at-risk populations in relation to crime and public safety, education, employment, health and early mortality. In many communities, these young men are more likely to be killed in gang- or family-related violence than they are to graduate from college.

According to social scientists such as New York University Professor Pedro Noguera and his colleagues, who recently co-edited *Invisible No More: Understanding the Disenfranchisement of Latino Men and Boys* (Routledge, 2012), Latino males in the United States are confronted with a wide variety of hardships. They are populating prisons, dropping out of school and becoming overrepresented in low-paying service jobs at alarming rates. Young Latino men, especially, earn among the lowest wages in the country; they also experience a rapidly growing rate of HIV/AIDS and one of the highest mortality rates due to homicide. Nevertheless, our experiences over the years working with and around these young men, as well as their families and their communities, inform an enduring sense of untapped potential, a longing for something better and real possibilities for redemption. What is needed and missing is a more serious societal investment in these young men, enlightened and culturally rooted interventions to help them chart a more constructive course and accessible opportunities to work, earn a living and contribute to the larger society.

We know from our own field experience and study that there exist important emerging intervention models showing real impact in shaping a more positive life course for Latino men and boys who have struggled in our various systems of education, employment and justice. We also know that the pathologies that disproportionately incline Latino men and boys to drop out of school, join gangs and engage in criminal activity are typically systemic. This is not to say that young Latino men who engage in violence and antisocial behavior should be exonerated; rather, it is merely to acknowledge that such proclivities are not generally inherent in such individuals. More often than not, they are the product of their family's socioeconomic circumstance, institutionalized racial inequality and misplaced public anxiety about young men of color generally in America.

Despite these realities and important recent research on the issues by leading Latino intellectuals, such as Professor Noguera, Professor Manuel Pastor of the University of Southern California and Professor Victor B. Sáenz of the University of Texas at El Paso, there remains a relative lack of research and scholarly work available on Latino men and boys, their unmet needs and program models that address these issues. *Overcoming Disparity: Latino Young Men and Boys* includes a bibliography assembled by University of California, Berkeley, scholar and Insight Center research consultant Ricardo Huerta Niño. It reflects the most salient works we could identify on contemporary issues related to Latino men and boys and includes an accompanying analysis of lingering gaps in the research that warrant immediate and meaningful investigation.

The balance of content that follows focuses on specific leaders and organizations across California and the Southwestern United States that have achieved deserved attention for producing impressively positive results with and for Latino men and boys—especially those individuals who have closely engaged with often hostile and impersonal public health and welfare, education and criminal justice systems. While each of these successful organizational and program models is distinct in its own right, there are common culturally based perspectives, practices and characteristics that connect them. Together these constitute what we refer to here as the *La Cultura Cura* (the Healing Culture) model. Typically, successful organizations and programs build on a combination of efforts involving culturally focused education and awareness, applied learning, community building activities and social enterprise. The most successful models and programs are often led and staffed by individuals who themselves have been at-risk school dropouts, gang members, substance abusers and criminals— individuals who have been there and done that, yet emerged from it better off for having ultimately decided to take a more positive and sustainable path. These kinds of organizational and program principals create unique bonds of trust, legitimacy and respect with the young participants who are intended to learn and benefit from them, based on parallel past experiences and lessons.

Most importantly, perhaps, leading organizations and programs operating in this space share a world view that sees the enduring value of redemption and rehabilitation—the foundational (though too often increasingly forgotten) principles of our nation's correctional system. Conversely, they also share a growing concern about the nation's increasingly punitive justice system, which often seems to be designed precisely to expand, rather than reduce, the scope of Latino and other minority males' incarceration prospects.

We acknowledge that the geographical focus of this work and the historical service constituencies most involved substantially weigh the voices and perspectives highlighted herein toward the particular experiences of Southwestern US Mexican American males. However, we firmly believe the book's contents promoting cultural proficiency are relevant to the analogous experiences of Latino men and boys of other ethnic backgrounds and individuals from other parts of California and the nation who are also heavily affected by the issues. These include members of America's fast-growing Salvadoran/Central American communities and non-Spanish-speaking indigenous populations from rural Mexico and Central America; the large Caribbean populations of the northeastern United States that are comprised mainly of Puerto Ricans and Dominicans; and the Midwest's large and growing cohorts of all of these Latino sub-groups.

The pages that follow also contain important reference materials. These include, in addition to the bibliography referenced earlier: (1) various informing statements, curricula, evaluations and publications that top-performing organizations and leaders in this space have produced over the years; (2) references to tools and best practices that these groups and practitioners have effectively employed; and (3) contact information on the specific leaders and organizations featured, as well as their allies and others who are actively engaged in this work.

We are most grateful to the various colleagues who contributed to this volume's publication, including especially the various field executives and organizations whose leadership produced the content featured here. We also owe special gratitude to our many generous funding partners, whose financial support made this volume and allied activities possible. These include the California Community Foundation, the California Endowment, the Marguerite Casey Foundation, the Sierra Health Foundation and the W. K. Kellogg Foundation. We appreciate the forward thinking of these leading social investment institutions and their shared commitment to advancing democracy and inclusion in America.

Finally, we would be remiss not to underscore our special gratitude to the volume's publisher, Dr. Nicolás Kanellos of the University of Houston, and his impressive team at Arte Público Press. In this connection, the able editorial collaboration of Dr. Gabriela Baeza Ventura is particularly appreciated.

Through publications like this one and others we have produced in this series, we believe American policy and national investment strategy can be greatly improved in future years. We thus urge you to share this book with your colleagues and friends and to become a more active participant in public discussions and initiatives intended to expand awareness of the issues and support for the kinds of affirmative investments and solutions presented herein.

Foreword

Daniel "Nane" Alejandrez

I am honored to be asked to provide some forwarding comments for this important publication addressing a crucial
national priority: the caring, healing, welfare and nurturing of
Latino boys and men. First, I must offer all honor and respect
to the Creator, our ancestors, families and circle of relations
for allowing me to share these words. I offer a prayer as well for
all in our community who suffer from lingering poverty and
those who have been incarcerated unjustly or lost loved ones
to community violence. America is at a critical juncture in its
history. For every step forward that this country takes toward
advancing justice, creating equality of opportunity and
becoming a tolerant nation that embraces its pluralism, there
are egregious remnant injustices, discrimination and incidents
of racism that remind us we still have work to do.

Eight years ago, the election of Barack Obama represented a
watershed moment for advancements in race and democracy.
Like many of us who have felt the sting of poverty and racism in
our lifetimes, I wept and was filled with new hope. The eupho-
ria and sense of "victory" were short-lived, however. Almost
immediately, the conservative backlash (i.e., organized and cat-
egorical resistance, if not blatant, unreasonable noncooperation)
by conservatives in Congress and the media was fierce, and
political rhetoric along the racial divide quickly became as pro-

nounced as ever. The schism was especially true in areas of the most urgently needed social reform: alleviating poverty, the correction of pronounced disparities in education and health and the disproportionate representation in the justice system for communities of color. We should be grateful for milestone advances in health-care reform, slowly raising the minimum wage, elevating rights for the LGBT community, executive order protections for immigrant parents of native born children, symbolically ending the war in Iraq and ostensibly fending off collapse of the US financial system (blessing or curse?).

The high hopes for accelerated national transformation spurred by the Barack Obama inauguration steadily faded to accepting the hard realities of having to achieve social change via sustained organizing, demonstrations and advocacy by poor communities of color. In 2007, looking back prior to the emergence of a viable Obama candidacy or the existence of an identifiable field of interest called "boys and men of color" (BMoC), Frank de Jesús Acosta wrote a book entitled, *The History of Barrios Unidos: Healing Community Violence, Cultura Es Cura*. The book tells the story of how Barrios Unidos harnessed the power of culture and spirituality to rescue and restore imperiled young lives, provide avenues to quell gang warfare and offer a promising model for building healthy and vibrant multicultural communities. Also, elders of the movement, such as Dolores Huerta, Harry Belafonte, Tom Hayden, Connie Rice and Professor Manuel Pastor, offered some suggestions for the contemporary agenda of civil rights that seem to be more urgent than ever.[1]

When asked to comment on civil rights priorities for changing the disparities faced by at-risk Latino children, youth and families, Dolores Huerta pointed out that disparity is linked to

---

[1]Frank de Jesús Acosta, *The History of Barrios Unidos: Healing Community Violence, Cultura Es Cura* (Houston: Arte Público Press, 2007).

the unfinished business of the struggle: namely, the structural eradication of poverty in America. "Poverty," she proclaimed, "will not go anywhere unless people engage in sustained organizing. The path to ending poverty and achieving the broader unfulfilled aims of civil rights cuts across the many fronts of economics, education, health, housing, environment, criminal and juvenile justice, political representation, civil liberties and race relations, rendering it important to prepare for a long-term nonviolent campaign. Education will prove to be the great equalizer. Organizing for social change demands strengthening the fabric of our communities that have suffered so much harm from generations of oppression, discrimination and injustice."

Asked the same question, Harry Belafonte commented that "the prevalence of suffocating poverty and its attendant oppressions still defines daily existence for the majority of blacks, Latinos and Native Americans of this nation. We must acknowledge that it is counter to the principles of democracy to allow people to suffer the indignity and inhumanity of abject poverty. Furthermore, it is imperative to reform the justice system from top to bottom. The criminal courts are failing to serve a higher good and the public interest. . . . Levels of mass incarceration unprecedented in modern global civilization have decimated poor black and Latino communities through what amounts to social, political and economic genocide through the physical removal and disfranchisement of adults, young men, children and women from family and civic life."

In many ways, these comments by elders Huerta and Belafonte could be adopted as a preamble for any national effort to dismantle the "school-to-prison pipeline," as reflected in a 2014 report by the president's My Brothers' Keeper Initiative.

It is important to make the point that the emergence of the field of boys and men of color is the direct outgrowth of a few previous movements and related national initiatives. At the risk of biting the hand that feeds me and fellow social change advocates, I will say that public resources and private philanthropy tend to move from issue to issue before the job is done. Of course, as the above discourse points out, the BMoC dialogue is subsumed within any greater conversation of the unfinished business of civil rights. That said, there are two interrelated national (and international) initiatives that flourished with the support of public health (PH) philanthropy: the national gang truce movement and the public health-sponsored violence prevention movement (also known as the community peace movement).

The PH framework provided the umbrella for these efforts and most of the interdisciplinary, comprehensive and culturally based models featured in this publication as examples of best practice in BMoC. In fact, Santa Cruz Barrios Unidos, National Compadres Network, La Plazita Institute, Communities United for Restorative Youth Justice (CURYJ), Homies Unidos and Homeboys Industries are all considered best practice models in violence prevention as well. Many of the guiding values, principles, strategies and culturally proficient comprehensive modalities or community-based frameworks offered in this book series (particularly contemporary practices rooted in La Cultura Cura) were cultivated in violence prevention.

For the purpose of comparison and reference, I offer up some of the guiding principles, core strategies and recommendations for policy change, systems change and social investments pioneered in the violence prevention field over the past twenty-three years or so.

The Kansas City Peace Summit. In the aftermath of the 1992 civil unrest in Los Angeles, a truce that began between the primarily African American gangs known as the Crips and the Bloods in that city began to spread to other black gangs in cities across the country. Parallel truce efforts led by Barrios Unidos and the Coalition to End Barrio Warfare in Latino communities across California created a natural alliance. The Urban Peace and Justice Summit, held in Kansas City, Missouri, in 1993, has been called the first constitutional convention of the community peace movement in the United States. The idea of gathering leading gangs was to establish a national agenda for addressing violence and its causes. The brainchild of community organizer Carl Upchurch, the summit was intended to propel the urban peace movement into the national spotlight by helping to broker a national moratorium on gang violence while also working to fashion a public policy agenda to address the root causes of social and economic violence in America's cities.[2] The summit trumpeted in a new vision for the urban community peace movement, one that looked beyond myopic gang prevention and intervention suppression strategies to promote instead a comprehensive social change agenda intended to increase public and private investment in the nation's minority youth.

The gathering coincided with the then-emerging field of violence prevention which sought to tackle the root causes of violence, such as poverty, injustice and the ongoing manifestations of institutionalized racism.[3] The summit's major conclusions and proposals for responsive initiatives reflected this collective wisdom and are still relevant to the community peace movement (and boys and men of color) today. In effect, summit proposals called for:

- Public and private investment in community-based education and youth development initiatives that pro-

---

[2]Carl Upchurch, *Convicted in the Womb* (New York: Bantam Books, 1996).
[3]*Health Affairs*, Winter 1993.

mote self-determination, character development, cultural understanding, leadership, academic achievement, skills building and responsible social involvement.

- Restoration of public funding for parks and recreation, as well as after-school and cultural programs serving children and youth in poor communities.
- Economic development efforts that include employment, small business financing, affordable housing and more accessible health and human services.[4]
- Organizing to oppose federal and state "three strikes" legislation, which mandates maximum prison sentences for multiple offenders, and the sentencing treatment of multiple misdemeanor offenders as felons.
- Public policy advocacy to rescind antigang programs, such as the federally supported Weed and Seed Initiative.
- Adoption of a major national initiative to comprehensively address the root causes of violence in its various forms across the nation, including gang violence, domestic violence, sexual assault and child abuse.
- Public education campaigns to shift the trend of national sentiment and policies leading to the criminalization and demonization of poor youth and young men of color.

The Barrios Unidos César Chávez Peace Plan. During 1995 and 1996, Barrios Unidos organized a series of four peace and unity summits in Santa Cruz, El Paso, San Antonio and Washington, DC, that led to the conceptualization and adoption of the five-point César Chávez Peace Plan (CCPP). The focus of the summits was to fashion a national violence prevention agenda that drew from the best thinking emerging in

---

[4]The summit participants particularly called for immediate federal legislation to provide 500,000 jobs for at-risk youth and young adults in economically depressed communities.

the country at that time in fields ranging from public health and juvenile justice to youth development and community building. The César Chávez Peace Plan has been used as a strategic organizing platform to promote and implement a peace process throughout California and other parts of the country. In order for the plan to work, we must include all segments of society, government, business, churches and other community institutions that share our vision for a new tomorrow. Addressing the issue of violence in our communities, the plan offers a broad national and community level framework of strategies to mobilize the full breadth of human, institutional, public and private resources toward realizing healthy and peaceful communities.

In April 1996, the five-part César Chávez Peace Plan was adopted by the National Coalition of Barrios Unidos at a Peace Summit in Washington, DC, and presented to the staffs of the White House and members of the US Congress. The plan called for:

- Federal and state support of community peace agreements and truces
- Broad national implementation of viable violence prevention models
- Creation of "barrio enterprise zones" for youth-centered community economic development
- National initiatives to create alternatives to incarceration, address the root causes of youth violence and prevent police brutality
- Development of a youth-centered network to build and distribute resources for violence prevention and social investment

The California Wellness Foundation invested $60 million over a ten-year period from 1992 to 2003 in its flagship Violence Prevention Initiative (VPI). An additional $10 million was invested in partnership by other leading California private foundations that informed this direction in social policy and investment, including: the California Endowment, the James Irvine Foundation, the Sierra Health Foundation, Alliance Healthcare, the S. H. Cowell Foundation, the Crail-Johnson Foundation and the David and Lucile Packard Foundation. In those years, homicide was a leading cause of death of all young people between twelve and twenty-four years of age, and it disproportionately impacted youth of color. The public health perspective took into consideration the concomitant forces that increase risk in communities, such as lack of access to jobs, poor educational systems, lack of health care and affordable housing, racism and discrimination. Prior approaches from the fields of criminal justice and medicine tended to focus on violence after the fact. The VPI framework provided an umbrella for multiple disciplines to align strategies and resources to address the root causes, along with a public education campaign focused on reducing access to handguns.

The philanthropic investment in violence prevention is greatly responsible for creating a legitimate field of interest. In fact, the public health framework for violence prevention, its language, concepts and strategies, have been widely adopted across many of the most successful public and private initiatives and multiple disciplines related to youth development, alternative full-service education programs, restorative juvenile and criminal justice, community-based law enforcement, gang intervention, family violence and wellness-based community building efforts. In communities where real change has taken hold, public health and human services departments often serve as the hubs for interdepartmental violence prevention resource alignment with community partners. All of the La Cultura Cura best practice models featured in this publication have worked within and helped to evolve the public health framework holistically, as it relates to culturally proficient comprehensive developmental efforts with at-risk youth, violence prevention, gang intervention, restorative justice work, community building, community economic enterprise or other modalities now labeled "boys and men of color."

One need only review the conclusions and recommendations set forth in the May 2014 *My Brother's Keeper Task Force Report to the President* to confirm the influence of public health and comprehensive philanthropic investment. Recommendations focus on such critical investment areas as access to safety net health and human service resources; educational readiness, retention and graduation; college access and vocational readiness; elimination of school suspension and expulsion practices and implementation of restorative supports; teen health and parent education; family violence prevention; restorative focused justice system and community partnerships; second-chance strategies for adults and juveniles involved with the justice system; transparent participatory research; and the use of evidence-based public health strategies.

Certainly, reforms in education and justice are desperately needed. At the same time, we are talking about needing staying power over the long haul in order to achieve sustainable reforms in policy, systems and private resource investments. The disparities created by intergenerational poverty, institutional racism, discrimination and recalcitrant inequalities are deeply rooted and condemn children and youth of color to poor life outcomes. The La Cultura Cura models offered in this book are not simply program modalities but long-term working values, principles, strategies and authentic ways of life demanding commitments to pluralism and justice in democratic social, political and economic practice.

The observations, perspectives and prescriptions presented throughout this book seek to improve the life outcomes for Latino boys and men of indigenous descent. There is no claim here that they comprise an all-inclusive or comprehensive panacea for all communities of color. We recognize that the best practice models have primarily been cultivated in the Southwest. However, the research, development and demonstration work of the National Compadres Network, in interculturally proficient modalities, to be offered through the proposed National Boys and Men of Color Institute, hold great promise.

Lastly, but equally important as anything I've expressed on these pages, let me state with the strongest urgency that without intimately including and involving boys and men who are presently incarcerated behind bars, any efforts to break the cycles of violence and incarceration will be compromised and doomed to fail. These boys and men on the inside are a central human agency elemental to establishing a viable and sustainable peace movement in high-risk outside communities. Truces, cease-fires, moratoriums on violence and recruitment of young ones into gangs or criminal affiliations can take hold only when they are involved. Fundamentally, incarcerated individuals on a restorative path are essential influences in prevention, intervention and reentry efforts to end the cycle in families and communities.

Ultimately, this book is written in the spirit of *In Lak'ech Hala Ken* ("I am the other you, and you are the other me"); offering an inclusive indigenous world view that values all life as sacred and considers the well-being of all communities. Ending disparity and attaining health are fundamentally interrelated; I cannot be whole unless you are whole. We are one interconnected body of humanity.

Introduction

Henry A. J. Ramos

For generations, gang culture and violence have defined the lived experience of Latino men and boys across much of the nation and especially the Southwestern United States. In the 1940s, pachucos, marginalized Mexican-American youth on the edges of criminality, first became a topic of national discourse. During a two-month-long period at the height of World War II, white sailors and soldiers stationed in Southern California engaged in a series of vigilante attacks on Mexican American youths sporting zoot suits, often worn by pachucos. These uniformed servicemen perceived the zoot-suiters as aliens within the boundaries of the United States during wartime. Instead of arresting and prosecuting these servicemen, the police arrested the Mexican American youths.

The violence resulting from what the media called the "Zoot Suit Riots" was broadly reported in the national press. In 1979, the tragic event in our nation's history was memorialized in Luis Valdez's play *Zoot Suit*. Valdez's play is notable for presenting a profoundly reflective, authentic and multidimensional account of the Latino male experience in America. But it is equally distinct for being one of the very few mainly positive and sympathetic media portrayals of Latino young men ever produced in the United States.

Sadly, for most of our history since World War II, Latino men and boys in the United States have been misunderstood by the majority of Americans, often because of their over-whelmingly negative portrayals in stage dramas, movies and other forms of popular culture. In the 1950s, for example, against the backdrop of Manhattan's West Side in New York City, Puerto Rican gangs were represented by the iconic, if nefarious, Sharks in the hit Broadway musical *West Side Story*, which was later immortalized in the Academy Award–winning film of the same title. The popular musical and movie represented both the Puerto Rican youths and their white gang counterparts, the Jets, as unwitting captives of a divisive American racial history born of generations of intergroup conflict resulting from each wave of immigration and demographic diversification. While the Puerto Rican youths aspired to gain respect, if not acceptance, in American culture, it was nevertheless clear throughout *West Side Story* that they would only be seen as foreigners and threats to the larger society.

In the late 1950s and early 1960s, Mexican-American and other Latino community leaders quietly began to assert their emerging political power in key electoral theaters, such as California, Illinois, New York and Texas. In large measure, they did this through expanded civil rights and community-building efforts led by young, emerging male leaders of groups such as the Latino-veterans-focused American GI Forum, the Mexican American Political Association, the Young Lords and the Mexican American Youth Organization. Veterans were an especially potent element of this success. Having fought for democracy abroad and sacrificed mightily in battle during World War II and the subsequent Korean conflict (Latino soldiers were among these conflicts' most decorated American combatants), these young veterans returned to the United

States to unfortunately face continuing racism and prejudice in their own nation.

The gains achieved by these leaders were groundbreaking. These included securing for the first time essential nationwide legal and policy victories for Latinos in criminal justice, education and labor through a series of federal and state court battles and federal legislative actions; many of these advances were pushed forward by concomitant political organizing and engagement. But, despite the impressive efforts of the World War II generation of Latino returning veterans, in the public domain and the major media, Spanish-speaking Americans—and especially Latino males—of all backgrounds continued to be perceived by mainstream institutions and observers intermittently as either hapless, tragic or dangerous figures.

In the 1956 movie *Giant*, for example, the Mexican American men featured are essentially portrayed as either poor, downtrodden manual laborers or wounded warriors whose only hope of gaining mainstream standing and respect is by fighting in overseas wars (often at the expense of their very lives). Similarly, in the 1962 movie *Requiem for a Heavyweight*, starring Mexican-born actor Anthony Quinn, the lead character, Mountain Rivera, is an aging and broken Latino boxer nearing the end of his career. The movie charts Rivera's fall from grace as a once-upon-a-time heavyweight championship contender on account of years of deception and mishandling on the part of his white business manager.

Later in the 1960s, Mexican-American youth demanded a different and more positive portrayal of their experiences and communities. They also began to critique key aspects of American civic culture. Like their counterparts in other racial and ethnic minority communities, and like the so-called hippie generation of young white Americans during that era, they asserted themselves in unprecedented ways to express profound disagreements with American social, economic, political and military policies of the day. They organized with the late, renowned farm labor leader César Chávez, who fought for economic justice in the agricultural fields of California and other Southwestern states. They vigorously protested against the Vietnam War and racial injustice and inequality in America. They organized to form progressive new vehicles to increase the participation of Spanish-speaking people in organized labor, politics, community economic development and the arts. And they consolidated assertive new public identities rooted in a resuscitation of pride in their indigenous origins.

Along with these developments in the 1960s emerged a new culture among Mexican-American youth, who came to self-identify as Chicanos. The term established a chosen, rather than societally imposed, reference point to harness the collective energies of many young Mexican Americans across the Southwest. Building on the historical remnants of pachuco culture and this new sense of shared identity and pride, a distinct new fusion and style of language, dress, iconography and comportment followed. Mexican-American men and boys were central drivers of these developments.

Notwithstanding the progressive, purposeful aims that many Chicano youths pursued during the 1960s and 1970s, a significant gang culture continued to affect numerous Mexican-American households and communities across California and the Southwest. Young Chicano males became increasingly implicated in gangs associated with criminal activity extending beyond mere turf skirmishes with rival groups. Criminal syndicates implicating large international drug cartels emerged and penetrated gang networks all across the region, resulting in growing numbers of Chicano young men being detained or incarcerated for criminal activities up to and including serious drug peddling, property and physical assault felonies, human trafficking and murder. Similar developments affected and shaped the experiences of other Latino males and groups across the United States from Chicago to New York and from Washington, DC to Miami.

By the 1980s, Chicano gang culture had begun to penetrate the national consciousness on a broader scale as a result of these developments and a new kind of projection of Mexican American male protagonists in popular movies, such as *Stand and Deliver* and *American Me*. Both movies, principally developed and produced by Latino filmmakers, feature leading Hollywood Mexican American icon Edward James Olmos in singular parts reflecting the two halves of the Chicano identity: on the one hand, *Stand and Deliver* was the uplifting story of a righteous educator working to help at-risk Chicano inner-city high school students achieve academic success and equality in America; and on the other hand, *American Me* presented a sympathetic, although brutally disturbing, depiction of a Chicano gang leader in California and his ultimately unsuccessful struggle for justice and redemption.

In addition to these popular perception-shaping images of young Latino men and boys in America, the 1980s produced the movie *Scarface*, featuring Italian American Academy Award winner Al Pacino depicting a Cuban refugee named Tony Montana. The film character Montana concluded that his only pathway to success and respect in America was through violence, greed and dealing. He accordingly assumed a life of crime and killing to gain acceptance and standing in US culture. Unfortunately, the character Tony Montana became for many Americans a personification of all the bad behavior and drug- and gang-related violence of Latinos. Popular images of a prototypical criminal predator emerged, generally associating him with violent gang- and drug-related crime. The confluence of expanding drug use and violence, on the one hand, and growing negative public perceptions of minority youth's role in creating these problems, on the other hand, persuaded too many US voters to support massive changes in law and policy leading to a radical increase in punitive criminal sentencing among Latino and other young men of color beginning in the 1990s.

Public concern about growing crime and violence in America was not entirely misplaced. Indeed, the 1980s had produced disturbing new increases in crime and especially violent crime associated with gang activity all across the nation, largely as a result of the growing popularity of crack cocaine in many American cities and the relative absence of legitimate economic opportunities for poor youth of color. What was problematic, however, from a long-term perspective was the public's exaggerated response. By the mid-1990s, many states began to adopt increasingly punitive penal regimes. California largely led the way in this direction. According to law professors Jennifer Lynn-Whaley and Andrea Russi of the University of California, Berkeley:

> In the late-1980s when violent crime was on the rise, and notably juvenile violent crime, politicians responded to growing public anxiety by becoming increasingly "tough on crime" in their campaign rhetoric and legislative agendas. Between 1987 and 1993, the dramatic increase in juvenile crime was evidenced by spikes in nearly every violent crime category, and underscored by a 65% increase in juvenile homicides. . . . While the majority of the nation responded to the panic surrounding the spike in juvenile violent crime by passing crime bills that toughened sanctions against

juveniles, California set the bar, pushing punitive juvenile policy further than any state.[1]

Throughout the 1990s, invoking a series of draconian policy measures, California criminal justice policies were hardened by voter demands to include such practices as "three strikes" multiple offender penalties, mandatory minimum sentences, the trial of minors as adults for (even first-time) serious offenses and major investments in the building of new prison facilities to support the resulting mass incarceration of young Latinos and other men and boys of color across the state. A primary thrust of this policy trend was increasingly to invoke adult penalties and consequences in the apprehension, prosecution and sentencing of minor youth accused of criminal activity.

Other states followed suit, and by the close of the twentieth century, every state with the exception of three had modified their laws to make it easier to try youthful offenders in adult courts. As Lynn-Whaley and Russi reported, this radically changed the culture of criminal justice in America: "the architects of juvenile justice policy began shifting away from the long-standing focus on rehabilitation to mirror the more punitive corrections strategies that originated in the adult criminal justice system years earlier."

As a result, the state's and the nation's detention populations ballooned over subsequent years. In fact, according to a 2010 report by the University of California-based Berkeley Center for Criminal Justice, between 1980 and 2009, California's prison population increased by nearly 600 percent. Lati-

---

[1]Jennifer Lynn-Whaley and Andrea Russi, *Improving Juvenile Justice Policy in California: A Closer Look at Transfer Laws' Impact on Young Men & Boys of Color* Warren Institute on Law and Social Policy (University of California: Berkeley, August 2011).

nos and African Americans, in turn, were overwhelmingly implicated. In many instances, selective law enforcement and financial incentives to warehouse men and boys of color were further enhanced by the use and reinforcing lobbying powers of white-owned private sector vendors seeking to build their businesses through expanded state contracting agreements to manage correctional facilities, security staffs and allied procurement programs or to "hire" inmates for production labor at sub-minimum-wage payment levels.

Racial disparities in prison demographics, sentencing and the transfer of youths to adult prison facilities intensified throughout California during this period, as the impacts of the shift to more punitive than restorative policies and practices grew over time. According to Lynn-Whaley and Rossi, writing in 2009:

> Youth of color, particularly African-American and Latino youth, are more likely to have contact with the juvenile justice system than white youth. This impact is greater at all stages, from arrest to confinement. Research shows that these youth experience a "cumulative disadvantage" as they move along the pipeline from arrest to incarceration. For example, in California, youth of color represent 65% of the overall youth population but 84% of youth in detention.

The racial inequities and dimensionalities of expanding incarceration across the nation have been equally disturbing where men and boys of color are concerned. According to the Sentencing Project, today in America nearly 60% of middle-aged African American men without a high school degree have served time in prison. And while blacks and Latinos together comprise 30% of the general population, they account for 58% of prisoners. Criminal justice policies and practices, and not just crime rates, are key drivers of these trends: correctional populations have grown during periods of declining crime rates and people of color are disproportionately punished for crimes that they commit at higher rates than whites. In fact, according to additional Sentencing Project data, African American men are now six times more likely and Latino men nearly three times more likely than white men to be in prison.

The growing racialization and the increasingly punitive nature of California and national corrections policies have serious implications for the future of American democratic integrity, social harmony and global competitiveness. International human rights organizations and such networks as the United Nations Working Group on Arbitrary Detention, Amnesty International and the Centre for Research on Globalization have criticized both the state of California and the United States during recent years for housing among the world's largest per capita prison populations and for supporting grossly inequitable practices leading to racial disparities in incarceration and sentencing that contradict our national claims of democratic governance and fairness.

By a large measure, the United States houses the world's largest prison population. While the US total population comprises only 4.4 percent of the world's overall population, it houses 22 percent of the world's prisoners. In 2013 in the United States, there were 698 people incarcerated per 100,000 members of the population. Comparing some countries with similar percentages of immigrants, one sees immediately how relatively aggressive American penal law is by world standards. Germany has an incarceration rate of only 76 individuals per 100,000 people (as of 2014). Italy incarcerates 85 of its citizens per 100,000 (as of 2015). Saudi Arabia incarcerates 161 out of every 100,000 of its people (as of 2013). If we compare other countries with a zero tolerance policy for illegal drugs, we see the incarceration rate for Russia is 455 per 100,000 (as of 2015). For Kazakhstan, the incarceration rate is 275 per 100,000 (as of 2015). In Singapore, it is 220 per 100,000 (as of 2014); and in Sweden, the rate is 60 individuals per 100,000 (as of 2014).

Recent years have seen important decreases in the California and national prison population, although more recent data, starting in 2013, show a slowing of this trend. Part of this phenomenon in states like California has been due to voter reassessment of the merits and efficacy of housing such large and quasi-permanent cadres of prisoners, especially given the costs and the increasingly glaring racial disparities involved in contemporary correctional systems management. Experts estimate that it now costs American taxpayers about $75 billion annually to support prisoners in detention. Moreover, applied research has increasingly cast doubt on the correlation between high incarceration rates and enhanced public safety, despite the fact that national crime rates—especially for serious offenses—have been on the decline for the most part. For example, according to a 2004 Bureau of Justice Statistics study, despite the total number of prisoners incarcerated for drug-related offenses increasing by 57,000 between 1997 and 2004, the proportion of drug offenders to total prisoners in state prison populations stayed steady at 21 percent. In effect, the data reveal that harsher criminal offense laws and sentencing regimes have had a negligible effect on serious drug-related criminal activity.

The penalization of youth and race that has effectively resulted from recent decades of systematically biased criminal and gang prevention policies in America has further laid a dangerous foundation for continued and growing intergroup conflict in the United States. The history of social conflict in our nation resulting from systemic racial discrimination and its vestiges has been well documented. But our recent spate of renewed racial tensions owing to the last several years' growing incidence of police brutality and killings of unarmed people of color has raised the specter of a potential for minority community backlash that has dangerous national security implications.

Americans tend to feel that we are somehow exempt from the dynamics of extreme poverty and political dislocation that create terrorist networks and violence in less developed nations. However, it is entirely conceivable that if we do not improve our policy soon, our growing population of disengaged and disenchanted minority youth will resort to organized efforts to express their political and economic discontent through large-scale violence. The conditions for such extremism are sadly already in motion. Latino and other diverse American groups living in varying levels of poverty and sociopolitical disadvantage constitute the most significant growth segments of our fast-changing national population. This scenario is not to raise the notion that poor Latinos and African American young men have some inherent propensity for violence or represent the threat of a powder keg ready to explode. But if history has taught us anything, it is that oppressed people will rise up in organized dissent and protest in the face of recalcitrant injustice.

By 2050 it is estimated that fully one-quarter of America's population will be comprised of Latinos. Another 25 percent will be comprised of diverse groups of African, Asian, and Middle Eastern immigrants and refugees and their offspring. With continuing trajectories of severe socioeconomic, educational, employment, health and justice challenges, the incentives for these groups to accept the status quo as we now know it will diminish considerably over time. Latinos will continue overwhelmingly to constitute the largest population cohort reshaping our national population landscape in years to come. Left unchecked, continued limited opportunities and social investments available to Latino Americans and similar groups will leave doors wide open for disaffected Latino and other youth to align even further with the international cartels and paramilitary organizations that already influence much of America's international trade in weapons, drugs and human trafficking.

The net effect of such developments would include expanded public violence in America not unlike what past decades have seen in countries such as Colombia and Mexico, or various nations in Asia and the Middle East, which have been subject to prolonged social cleavages and associated terrorist activity. The costs to our society, military and law enforcement agencies to contain such developments would dwarf our current security expenditures; and the cost in lost human life and property would be untenable. As importantly, the costs to our democracy and social fabric, indeed to our shared identity as Americans, would suffer severely in response to such a decline in social harmony resulting from staying on the path we have been on in recent years.

Finally, given the demographic trends just discussed, our economic viability and competitiveness as a nation hangs in the balance. Prolonged disparity, overt injustice and de facto sanctioned discrimination can only breed desperation, growing frustration and alienation from society. Given that so many Latino and other young men of color are being systematically relegated to lives of crime and violence by severely limited life choices, and given that these young men comprise among the fastest growing segments of our national population, it is impossible to imagine how the America of the future can succeed without these young men succeeding as well. In no more than a quarter century, virtually every village and hamlet across the land will be inhabited by robust and growing populations of Latino American individuals and families. There will be no place in America that is not affected by the plight or the increasing success of Latino and other groups of color.

Young Latino men in this trajectory either can become agents of progress and socioeconomic advancement, or they can become more mired in antisocial, unproductive and violent behaviors. In the first instance, the Latino youth of tomorrow will be net contributors to American economy, society and culture. In the second instance, they will be even more significant economic and emotional drains on the rest of society—that is, long-term cost centers whose failures diminish all of us and our prospects for broadly shared prosperity and community peace.

Let's speak frankly: poverty, failing schools and prisons are the face of American democratic failure. In America we can and we must do better. Across the nation's fast-growing Latino communities there are numerous proven leaders, and models of prevention and intervention, whose work and ideas portend far better outcomes for our youth and young adults than the status quo is producing—if only we can sufficiently support their replication, scaling and sustainability. In short, while there are undeniably vast problems to be addressed where at-risk Latino men and boys are concerned, even more importantly, we must also recognize a growing number of solutions, tools and resources are becoming available to US policy leaders of integrity who are sincerely committed to ensuring the success of these young people and, in the process, a more bright, profitable and harmonious American future.

This book is intended to highlight some of the leading solutions, tools and resources that have emerged in recent years to address both challenges and opportunities related to the issues. The featured technologies, programs and practices build largely on the culturally grounded La Cultura Cura (Culture of Healing) model of community engagement and self-help practice that we highlighted in our earlier book, *The History of Barrios Unidos*. Based in Santa Cruz, California, Barrios Unidos (Spanish for "United Neighborhoods") is the creator of cutting-edge grassroots education, service and social enterprise programs that have helped to pioneer efforts and progress in this space for more than three decades.

At the core of this work has been an emphasis on Chicano/Latino history, the use of cultural expression and ritual as sources of community education and self-awareness, the development of active community volunteer programs designed to improve neighborhood conditions and the advancement of supporting socially focused business ventures that encourage youth and community economic development. Other vital aspects of this work are the building of common bonds with other groups of Latino/minority youth change agents and the building of social and organizing bonds with other progressive racial and ethnic groups working on social and economic justice issues.

In this volume, we seek to lift up the work and lessons of two additional leading Southwest-focused prevention and intervention models designed to enhance the healthy formation and life success of low-income, at-risk Latino men and boys. These allied efforts are, respectively, the California-based National Compadres Network, whose focus is promoting the positive involvement of Latino males in the lives of their families, communities and society; and La Plazita Institute, a grassroots nonprofit organization based in Albuquerque, New Mexico, that utilizes the philosophy of La Cultura Cura to help Latino, Chicano and Native American youth and communities, drawing on their own roots and histories to express core traditional values of respect, honor, love and family in their public and private lives.

The book offers a combination of analyses based on extensive interviews with these organizations' principals, a curated sampling of the leading tools, practice models and impact evaluations they (or their close allies) have produced and a bibliographic review and comment on the current state of research on at-risk Latino men and boys. Its contents provide an essential current touch point for all manner of policy practitioners, community builders, social investors, applied researchers and media professionals concerned about American social policy, economy and intergroup relations.

Among the essential commonalities in the advancement of this vital and timely work is the intentionality of all these efforts to produce desired improvements in individual and community life quality and their commitment to utilizing indigenous cultural healing practices that seek to connect program and community participants to a higher calling than more conventional, mainstream program interventions are able to achieve. One of the principal shared touch points of these leaders' work has been their frequent use of art and creative expression to enable young people to find their authentic voices in the public domain. Using first-person spoken word, written poetry and prose, original drawings and paintings and tattoo art, among other creative forms, these programs have served to introduce young people across America to the untapped powers that reside within them and that, properly harnessed, can be of great service to their communities and the larger society.

Another shared aspect of these models' success has been the long continuity and proven leadership of the respective organization and network leaders who have developed and perfected them over the decades. Jerry Tello of the National Compadres Network, for example, has been engaged at the forefront of community study and healing work with Latino and other at-risk youth for nearly forty years. Through the example of his own family love, continuity and community service, his consistent authenticity and his unbending commitment to helping young people embrace their families and culture, their social responsibilities and their faith, Tello has provided unusual role modeling and guidance for thousands of young Latino and other at-risk youth over many years all across the United States. In addition, perhaps largely on account of his long perspective on the work still to be done, Tello and his colleagues at the National Compadres Network have been consistently leading practitioners in comprehensively documenting effective community-based practice in the field. The network is thus one of the still relatively few Latino-centric operations of its kind that can authentically claim it is guided by an evidence-based approach.

Many of the foremost leaders in this space are themselves formerly challenged youth who were involved in gang life and culture before they chose the path of peace and healing. Daniel "Nane" Alejandrez of Barrios Unidos exemplifies this experience. A former gang member and drug addict, Alejandrez lost two of his own brothers to gang violence and multiple family members to incarceration before he was inspired to chart a new course in his own life after hearing a speech by the late iconic farm labor organizer César Chávez. Alejandrez, who is the author of this volume's foreword, carries first-hand experience and street credibility of special relevance to the various young people Barrios Unidos engages, precisely on account of his own experience in the educational, criminal justice and public health systems that most implicate and negate the life prospects of Latino youth.

Similarly, Albino García, Jr., the principal of La Plazita Institute, struggled throughout his youth and early adulthood before he found the way to his current calling as one of the nation's leading youth and community empowerment advocates. García, who is half Mexican American and half Native American, stumbled through much of his youth, largely disconnected from his ethnic and indigenous roots. He faced constant struggles with substance abuse and the law. When he fell upon the opportunity to reconnect with his authentic self through a rediscovery of his roots, however, everything changed. According to a recent profile on the Indian Country Media Network:

> García's family was from northern New Mexico, but he grew up on the streets of Chicago. There, he descended into a life of alcohol abuse, drugs and gang violence. A couple of influences showed him that there could be another way. There was a stint with the Army in Korea, and he was young when he met Frances, the woman who became his wife. But the pull of the low life was so strong that he couldn't clean up. Even as his kids were small, he was in and out of jails and drug rehab programs. Ultimately, the lifeline that delivered García to a better way was not a job, his children or even true love. It was his long-forgotten identity as a Native American.[1]

For García, like Alejandrez, the rediscovery of his indigenous roots, a profound desire to overcome painful past

---

[1] A. Minard, "La Plazita Builds Native Pride Through Healing and Hard Work," Indian Country Media Network, September 10, 2013, http://indiancountrytodaymedianetwork.com/2013/09/10/la-plazita-rebuilds-native-pride-through-healing-and-hard-work-151216.

loss and the opportunity to work with and help young people who had inherited or taken dark paths via life on the streets became the rallying cry for his own redemption.

Leaders, organizations and programs like those featured here have been essential elements of resilience and survival in violence-torn communities across the Southwest and the rest of the nation. The work and commitment over the years point the way to a more ethical and effective manner of advancing justice in America. What these harbingers of needed change all share is a strong and abiding commitment to restorative justice models that maintain the focus of prevention and intervention efforts on the individual's rehabilitation and capacity to re-engage in society as a productive and valued contributor to the common good. They fundamentally reject, as we all should, the draconian and manifestly failed policies of punitive justice approaches, such as those that have dominated the American landscape for the past quarter century.

At its best, American policy has always been strongest and most effective when practical considerations have met with our highest ideals. For the better part of three decades now, California and other states have pursued justice with a very heavy ideological hand, one that has been especially tilted against the interests of poor people of color. Young men of color have been the principal targets and victims of this preferred policy approach, at a great ethical and financial expense to our country. In the process, we have jettisoned our long-standing commitment to criminal rehabilitation, one of the hallmarks of our civic culture throughout the modern age of our existence as a nation.

Now is the time for more realistic and measured policies that recognize the humanity in all of our nation's people, whatever their racial, ethnic, social, political or economic persuasion. Now is the time for a more reasoned recognition of the major opportunity costs we are paying as a society by investing in these young peoples' failure, as opposed to their success. Now is the time for a different course, one that builds on proven models and approaches like those featured here and in our predating analyses and reporting of the issues.

The very sustainability of American civic culture and global leadership hangs in the balance. In the future that awaits us, it will become increasingly difficult for America to maintain its cultural, political and economic leadership in the world without dramatically changing the course of our policy on youth violence and incarceration. In the absence of change, massive new public and private expenditures will be required to maintain peace on the streets of our cities and a minimal semblance of the order that is required for national productivity and competitiveness.

Along with reforms in law and social investment practice, we will also have to advance needed changes in the ways that we portray and think about Latino and other at-risk young men of color across America—in our mass media, in our workplace projections of their economic capabilities and in their presence in important publications, like this one, that are intended to educate and inform key decision makers in various fields of influence. It is only right that we move more humanely in these directions. After all, notwithstanding popular perceptions of these young men as predators who are deserving of punitive responses to their often antisocial behaviors, in fact, even with their sometimes criminal impulses and actions, they are themselves victims of systems of racial bias that often guide them to precisely the places we punish them most aggressively for going to.

Frequently these young men are children (some of them as young as fourteen years of age) being treated and tried as adults, both in the court of law and in the court of public opinion. For our society to be successful in the future that awaits us, what these young men need is love and care, investment and opportunity. It is the responsibility of all Americans, especially those who are among the most privileged in our midst, to stand up for a new and better way. It is critical to the future vitality of our democracy, our economy and our national well-being that Americans of all backgrounds join hands in this timely campaign with a collective commitment to change. The alternative can only be an unhappy fate for our nation, one for which the current generation of American adults should not want history to judge them as responsible parties.

CHAPTER 1

Latino Boys and Men: Assessing the State of Research and Practice

Ricardo Huerta Niño, PhD

Throughout various disciplines, scholars who write about Latino boys and men note the abundance of research and reporting on the dire conditions and statistics related to the state of the demographic. Many also emphasize the critical need for more research that highlights best practices for helping Latino boys and men remain on or return to a path of success. The aim of this brief assessment and accompanying bibliography is to provide scholars, practitioners, community members, funders and Latino boys and men themselves with a helpful resource.

The bibliography features research and reports on a variety of approaches, models and best practices for supporting Latino boys and men. It presents a solid body of knowledge documenting work and research focused on the key institutions and systems Latino boys and men are involved in. These include criminal justice and violence prevention, education, foster care, health care and youth development. The solution-oriented approaches represented in these works include frameworks emphasizing culture, identity, resilience, social capital, organization, mentoring, community development and youth development; asset-based methods; family-based approaches; and in some cases multiple-emphasis models.

The current review does not pretend to offer an exhaustive list of all the research and reports on the issues, nor is it fully comprehensive in terms of the categories featured. Such an endeavor is beyond the purpose and scope of the present work. Instead, the sections below reflect the results of targeted research on effective strategies for supporting Latino boys and men in major institutions and systems and the factors that hinder or promote their well-being and success. The effort aims to highlight where there exists laudable and abundant research, as well as where there remain glaring gaps in research that should be the priority of leading field researchers to address.

Some readers will note the absence of older, well-known research and publications. This is because a number of political, social, demographic and economic shifts in recent years require a new scholarship that reflects these new realties for Latino boys and men. In particular, it seems that the present period of slow but steady economic recovery provides an opportune moment for exploring what the research tells us about institutional strategies and best practices that optimally help Latino boys and men achieve better outcomes in areas ranging from education and workforce development to health and criminal justice. Given the goal of bringing together and examining the most current work in these areas, the review that follows focuses mainly on research produced in recent years.

The review also emphasizes research that disaggregates Latinos from other demographic groups. The rationale for focusing on Latino boys and men—separately from other racial and ethnic groups and separately from research on Latina girls and women—includes considerations for cultural, racial, regional and other differences in their particular experiences in institutions and systems. Several of the listed sources include these discussions.

It is important to note that various entries in the bibliography could have been listed under two or more subheadings and that other, further divisions could have been possible. However, for present purposes, we provide a more simplified framework for organizing the featured resources, grouping them by topic, as follows.

Criminal Justice and Violence Prevention

Research on criminal justice and violence prevention continues to be a real focus for scholars and practitioners. Given the statistics on incarceration rates for Latino boys and men, the abundance of research makes sense. Research interests in this category include topics on asset-based and family-based approaches to violence prevention. A subcategory of research in this space reflects urgent concerns related to discipline, surveillance, policing and the "school-to-prison pipeline." Some scholars examine the surveillance and discipline experiences of Latino boys in various contexts, most notably in schools, revealing the role of teachers and school leaders in these experiences. While some studies detail the challenges, others engage approaches for addressing those challenges, including the role educators play in developing alternatives to conventional instruction and policy.

An additional subcategory of research worth noting on this topic includes works that focus on models for prison recovery and reentry into society for former gang members and the formerly incarcerated, generally. This category of resources includes research examining efforts to help Latino males move away from lives of violence, as well as research on related issues of recovery and reentry into their families and society. In this category, known and proven models, such as one employed in various geographical settings across the nation by Victory Outreach, are examined. An overall assessment of the research on criminal justice and violence prevention indicates the need for a broader and richer body of research and reporting on best practices for Latino boys and men, as well as more coordinated efforts to bring together resources for both practitioners and applied researchers engaged in this work.

Education

Strong research on Latino boys and men in the education system is well represented in recent scholarship. Much of it emphasizes academic success models utilizing a variety of intervention strategies at different age-related entry points, from pre-K through college and university. Scholars are especially examining best practices that prioritize certain strategies to promote success, including, among others, mentoring, parent involvement and inculcation in a "college-going culture." These strategies call for adult interventions to provide students with a context for success.

In the subcategory of "Culture and Asset-based Approaches," scholars highlight educational best practices that are centered on the students. They emphasize the ways in which Latino boys and men are unique in their needs as well as their assets related to academic success. Models for helping Latino boys and men are centered on the strengths of their culture, on social capital between students and on using culturally responsive instruction and curricula.

While examples abound of good research in the area of education, there remains nevertheless a critical need for new studies on opportunities to enhance the educational success of young Latino men and boys. Scholars have additionally noted the great need for both research and practice to help address the many postcollege challenges facing Latino boys and men in the job market and at the workplace. They highlight the need to track the Latino professional pipeline development experience, in order to determine whether and what kinds of jobs they get, whether they are able to pay off their student loans and whether it is possible to quantify their postcollege experience in terms of how long it took to find a job, what their salary was, and how these metrics compare across race and ethnicity. The assumption that a college education leads to a good full-time job is not always the case for Latino college graduates.

Perhaps the most glaring absence in this area is scholarship and reporting on the academic experiences of Latino boys who are excelling academically and the strategies that facilitated their success. Overall, the research centers on students who are struggling or who have challenges that put them at risk of academic failure, highlighting best practices for supporting their recovery and ultimate success. A more complete picture of the educational experience of Latino boys and men would include case studies of those students who have managed to create their own strategies for success and would examine what lessons can be taken from those experiences.

Foster Care and Health

Surprisingly few resources exist in these two areas that focus specifically on best practices for helping Latino boys and men—a significant gap that should be of concern to scholars and practitioners, as well as the public and private funders that principally support policy research and development in the field. While there is plenty of research focused on Latino health problems, few resources exist highlighting practices, approaches or models that help Latino boys and men with their foster care experience or with achieving improved health outcomes. Compared to the relatively abundant available sources on best practices for Latino men and boys in education, the lists under these two categories clearly show a major gap in the research.

There is an urgent need to identify the strategies, approaches and models that have successfully helped Latino boys and men navigate these systems, provided opportunities for their success and led to more effective care. If we simply consider one of the most common health concerns for Latino boys and men, such as obesity, it is easy to imagine that there are programs across the country that are successfully engaging Latinos in promoting better health. Leading health funders, like several that have supported this publication's production (the California Endowment, W. K. Kellogg Foundation and Sierra Health Foundation) are increasingly supporting work in this arena. Further research is needed to identify the best models these investments are advancing and especially those that lend themselves to replication and scaling.

Youth Development

Several of the resources listed here examine models that include multiple strategies from various disciplines. While the resources in education, for example, tend to be limited to that field, sources under "Youth Development" involve broader discussions. In the broader context of this domain, it is clear there is a need for more synthetic work highlighting best practices across subject matter areas and disciplines. More comprehensive analyses would help to illuminate the relationship between, for instance, best practices in mental health and violence prevention in ways that could improve policy and practice. Multidisciplinary study of the issues can help to uniquely underscore the many dimensionalities of problems in ways that help to inform more coordinated investments and better outcomes. Finally, on a more localized level, more comprehensive analyses of the issues can inform more effective and community-responsive efforts intended to support Latino boys and men.

Resilience

This category of the review highlights resources and materials that examine the idea of resilience as a strategy for overcoming the many challenges and risks Latino men and boys face in areas like academic success and workforce development. The featured content examines how resiliency can be a factor in overcoming traditional hurdles to Latino male achievement in these and other areas. This research focuses on the individual's ability to survive and overcome challenges and on the role of adults (and especially parents) in fostering these and allied characteristics of resilience within their own and others' children.

Resiliency skeptics argue it could be harmful to burden already stressed Latino families with "personal responsibility" imperatives absent in corresponding institutional incentives and supports. This kind of analysis acknowledges the role of personal and family responsibility, or resilience, while also holding accountable the institutions and systems that are required to facilitate the well-being and success of Latino men and boys through responsive public policies and investments. Given still-divergent views on the efficacy of encouraging resilience as a priority strategy in public policy and social investment, it appears more investigation and assessment work is warranted in this area—especially work that reliably demonstrates the particular circumstances in which resilience-based approaches show measurable impacts and transferable benefits relative to Latino men and boys.

New Research Opportunities

Some of the resources listed in the bibliography are practitioner-based products explicitly focused on solution-oriented discussions of "what works." Many others are deep cross-cutting examinations of issues and problems by practitioners and applied researchers, and they often include related policy and strategy recommendations. There may exist many other resources like this that are not included in the present bibliography. Indeed, solutions supported by research and evidence are much in need in this space. Accordingly, in addition to there being a case for further and more cross-cutting research on models that work to improve the social and economic prospects of Latino men and boys in America, there is also an opportunity for scholars and practitioners to collaborate across disciplines on studies of mutual interest and to increase sharing and coordination around the discovery and promotion of research-informed best practices.

Too, more research is needed on subgroups within the broader category of Latino boys and men that can provide rich analysis and highlight best practices for specific subgroups. Further research could explore the ways in which policy recommendations can be adjusted to address the specific needs of LGBT, undocumented, rural or indigenous Latino boys and men. There is also a need for place-based analysis that would reveal how the health of Latino boys and men is affected, for example, by issues of environmental toxicity and would identify best practices for engaging young Latino males in response as community-based environmental justice organizers and activists.

Finally, there is a dire need for research that develops the body of knowledge around strategies, practices and models for Latino boys and men in economic development. The assumption in all the other categories discussed is that those efforts aim to prepare Latino boys and men to enter the workforce as gainfully employed workers making a living wage. However, the lack of research specific to what best supports this demographic seems to leave the field without a focused set of end goals or a clear methodology for successfully getting these boys and men into well-paying jobs.

Consequently, more study is needed on models that work to effectively engage leading national and regional employers in efforts to better train, place and advance young Latino males in good job and career pathways. Allied research is required to determine the best industry sectors to align with Latino male population distribution, growth and workforce preparation potential, in ways that dramatically increase the level of access young Latino males have to the best possible job opportunities they can qualify for. Last but not least, further study is needed on the best ways to successfully prepare and link Latino high school students to college degree programs in the STEM fields that are most likely to enhance their long-term employability, earnings and asset building potential.

Bibliography

I. Criminal Justice and Violence Prevention

Allison, Kevin W., Torey Edmonds, Karen Wilson, Michell Pope, and Albert D. Farrell. "Connecting Youth Violence Prevention, Positive Youth Development, and Community Mobilization." *American Journal of Community Psychology* 48.1–2 (2011): 8–20.

Haegerich, Tamara M., James Mercy, and Billie Weiss. "What Is the Role of Public Health in Gang-Membership Prevention?" *Changing Course* (2013): 31–50.

Kelly, Patricia J., Janna Lesser, An-Lin Cheng, Manuel Oscós-Sánchez, Elisabeth Martínez, Daniel Pineda, and Juan Mancha. "A Prospective Randomized Controlled Trial of an Interpersonal Violence Prevention Program With a Mexican American Community." *Family & Community Health* 33.3 (2010): 207–15.

Leap, Jorja, Todd M. Franke, Christina A. Christie, and Susana Bonis. "Nothing Stops a Bullet Like a Job: Homeboy

Industries Gang Prevention and Intervention in Los Angeles." In *Beyond Suppression: Global Perspectives on Youth Violence*, edited by Joan Serra Hoffman, Lyndee Knox, and Robert Cohen. Santa Barbara: Praeger, 2011. 127–38.

Leidy, Melinda S., Nancy G. Guerra, and Rosa I. Toro. "A Review of Family-Based Programs to Prevent Youth Violence Among Latinos." *Hispanic Journal of Behavioral Sciences* 32.1 (2010): 5–36.

Pastor, Manuel. "Keeping It Real: Demographic Change, Economic Conflict, and Inter-Ethnic Organizing for Social Justice in Los Angeles." In *Black and Brown in Los Angeles: Beyond Conflict and Coalition*, edited by Josh Kun and Laura Pulido. Berkeley: University of California Press, 2013. 33–66.

a. Prison Pipeline, Discipline and Policing

Fujimoto, Eugene, Yvonne García, Noemy Medina, and Eduardo Pérez. "Alternatives to the School-to-Prison Pipeline: The Role of Educational Leaders in Developing a College-Going Culture." *Association of Mexican-American Educators Journal* 7.3 (2013): 85–95.

Pantoja, Alicia. "Reframing the School-to-Prison Pipeline: The Experiences of Latin@ Youth and Families." *Association of Mexican American Educators Journal* 7.3 (2013): 17–31.

Pinnow, Rachel J. "An Ecology of Fear: Examining the Contradictory Surveillance Terrain Navigated by Mexican Youth in a US Middle School." *Anthropology & Education Quarterly* 44.3 (2013): 253–68.

Raible, John, and Jason G. Irizarry. "Redirecting the Teacher's Gaze: Teacher Education, Youth Surveillance and the School-to-Prison Pipeline." *Teaching and Teacher Education* 26.5 (2010): 1196–203.

Ríos, Víctor M., and Mario G. Galicia. "Smoking Guns or Smoke & Mirrors?: Schools and the Policing of Latino

Boys." *Association of Mexican American Educators Journal* 7.3 (2013): 54–66.

Skiba, Russell J., Robert H. Horner, Choong-Geun Chung, M. Karega Rausch, Seth L. May, and Tary Tobin. "Race Is Not Neutral: A National Investigation of African American and Latino Disproportionality in School Discipline." *School Psychology Review* 40.1 (2011): 85–107.

b. Community Reentry and Recovery

López-Aguado, Patrick. "Working Between Two Worlds: Gang Intervention and Street Liminality." *Ethnography* 14.2 (2013): 186–206.

Orozco Flores, Edward. "'I Am Somebody': Barrio Pentecostalism and Gendered Acculturation among Chicano Exgang Members." *Ethnic and Racial Studies* 32.6 (2009): 996–1016.

——. "Latinos and Faith-Based Recovery from Gangs." In *Sustaining Faith Traditions: Race, Ethnicity, and Religion among the Latino and Asian American Second Generation*, edited by Carolyn Chen and Russell Jeung, New York: NYU Press, 2012. 113–32.

——. *God's Gangs: Barrio Ministry, Masculinity, and Gang Recovery*. New York: NYU Press, 2013.

Orozco Flores, Edward, and Pierrette Hondagneu-Sotelo. "Chicano Gang Members in Recovery: The Public Talk of Negotiating Chicano Masculinities." *Social Problems* 60.4 (2013): 476–90.

II. Education

a. Academic Success

Alfaro, Edna C., Adriana J. Umaña-Taylor, Melinda A. Gonzales-Backen, Mayra Y. Bámaca, and Katharine H. Zeiders.

"Latino Adolescents' Academic Success: The Role of Discrimination, Academic Motivation, and Gender." *Journal of Adolescence* 32.4 (2009): 941–62.

Behnke, Andrew O., and Christine Kelly. "Creating Programs to Help Latino Youth Thrive at School: The Influence of Latino Parent Involvement Programs." *Journal of Extension* 49.1 (2011): 1–11.

Carrillo, Juan F. "The Unhomely in Academic Success: Latino Males Navigating the Ghetto Nerd Borderlands." *Culture, Society & Masculinities* 5.2 (2013): 193–207.

Conchas, Gilberto Q., Leticia Oseguera, and James Diego Vigil. "Acculturation and School Success: Understanding the Variability of Mexican American Youth Adaptation Across Urban and Suburban Contexts." *The Urban Review* 44.4 (2012): 401–22.

Crisp, Gloria, and Amaury Nora. "Hispanic Student Success: Factors Influencing the Persistence and Transfer Decisions of Latino Community College Students Enrolled in Developmental Education." *Research in Higher Education* 51.2 (2010): 175-94.

Dukakis, Kara, Nina Duong, Jorge Ruiz de Velasco, and Jamila Henderson. *College Access and Completion among Boys and Young Men of Color: Literature Review of Promising Practices.* Stanford, CA: Stanford University John W. Gardner Center for Youth and Their Communities, 2014.

Dumka, Larry E., Nancy A. Gonzales, Darya D. Bonds, and Roger E. Millsap. "Academic Success of Mexican Origin Adolescent Boys and Girls: The Role of Mothers' and Fathers' Parenting and Cultural Orientation." *Sex Roles* 60.7-8 (2009): 588–99.

Garrett, Tomás, René Antrop-González, and William Vélez. "Examining the Success Factors of High-Achieving Puerto

Rican Male High-School Students." *Roeper Review* 32.2 (2010): 106–15.

Harper, Shaun R., and Associates. *Succeeding in the City: A Report from the New York City Black and Latino Male High School Achievement Study.* Philadelphia: University of Pennsylvania, Center for the Study of Race and Equity in Education, 2014.

White House Initiative on Educational Excellence for Hispanics. *Hispanic Boys and Young Men Unlocking Their Full Potential to Benefit All Americans.* Washington, DC: US Department of Education, 2014.

Huerta, Adrián, and Seth Fishman. "Marginality and Mattering: Urban Latino Male Undergraduates in Higher Education." *Journal of the First-Year Experience & Students in Transition* 26.1 (2014): 85–100.

Jonas, Michael. "Study of Black and Latino Boys Excludes Charter Success." *Commonwealth Magazine*, April 2015.

LeFevre, Ann L., and Terry V. Shaw. "Latino Parent Involvement and School Success: Longitudinal Effects of Formal and Informal Support." *Education and Urban Society* 44.6 (2012): 707–23.

Lutz, Amy, and Stephanie Crist. "Why Do Bilingual Boys Get Better Grades in English-Only America? The Impacts of Gender, Language, and Family Interaction on Academic Achievement of Latino/a Children of Immigrants." *Ethnic and Racial Studies* 32.2 (2009): 346–68.

Noguera, Pedro A. "Saving Black and Latino Boys: What Schools Can Do to Make a Difference." *Education Week*, February 3, 2012.

Riegle Crumb, Catherine, and Rebecca M. Callahan. "Exploring the Academic Benefits of Friendship Ties for Latino Boys and Girls." *Social Science Quarterly* 90.3 (2009): 611–31.

Sáenz, Victor B., and Luis Ponjuan. "Men of Color: Ensuring the Academic Success of Latino Males in Higher Education." *Institute for Higher Education Policy* (2011).

Sánchez, Sheila M., Adrián H. Huerta, and Kristan M. Venegas. "Latino Males and College Preparation Programs: Examples of Increased Access." *Metropolitan Universities* 22.3 (2012): 27–45.

Woolley, Michael E. "Supporting School Completion Among Latino Youth: The Role of Adult Relationships." *Prevention Researcher* 16.3 (2009): 9–12.

Woolley, Michael E., Kelli L. Kol, and Gary L. Bowen. "The Social Context of School Success for Latino Middle School Students: Direct and Indirect Influences of Teachers, Family, and Friends." *The Journal of Early Adolescence* 29.1 (2009): 43-70.

b. Culture and Asset-Based Approaches

Advancing the Success of Boys and Men of Color in Education: Recommendations for Policymakers. Philadelphia: University of Pennsylvania, Center for the Study of Race and Equity in Education, 2015.

Campos, David. *Educating Latino Boys: An Asset-Based Approach.* Thousand Oaks, CA: Corwin Press, 2012.

Carrillo, Juan Fernando. "I Always Knew I Was Gifted: Latino Males and the Mestiz@ Theory of Intelligences (MTI)." *Berkeley Review of Education* 4.1 (2013): 69–95.

González, Juan Carlos, and Jason C. Immekus. "Experiences of Central California Latino Male Youth: Recollecting Despair and Success in Barrios and Schools." *Diaspora, Indigenous, and Minority Education: Studies of Migration, Integration, Equity, and Cultural Survival* 7.3 (2013): 180–97.

Hopkins, Megan, Mary Martínez Wenzl, Ursula S. Aldana, and Patricia Gándara. "Cultivating Capital: Latino Newcomer Young Men in a US Urban High School." *Anthropology & Education Quarterly* 44.3 (2013): 286–303.

Irizarry, Jason G., and John Raible. "Beginning with El Barrio: Learning from Exemplary Teachers of Latino Students." *Journal of Latinos and Education* 10.3 (2011): 186–203.

Rodríguez, Louie F. "The PUEDES Approach: A Paradigm for Understanding and Responding to the 21st Century Latina/o Dropout/Pushout Crisis in the US." *Journal of Critical Thought and Praxis* 2.1 (2013): 122–53.

Strayhorn, Terrell L. "When Race and Gender Collide: Social and Cultural Capital's Influence on the Academic Achievement of African American and Latino Males." *The Review of Higher Education* 33.3 (2010): 307–32.

Tung, Rosann, Vivian Dalila Carlo, Melissa Colón, Jaime L. Del Razo, John B. Diamond, Alethea Frazier Raynor, Daren Graves, Paul J. Kuttner, Helena Miranda, and Andresse St. Rose. *Promising Practices and Unfinished Business: Fostering Equity and Excellence for Black and Latino Males*. Providence, RI: Brown University, Annenberg Institute for School Reform, 2015.

III. Foster Care

Pérez, Beatrix F., and Harriett D. Romo. "'Couch Surfing' of Latino Foster Care Alumni: Reliance on Peers as Social Capital." *Journal of Adolescence* 34.2 (2011): 239–48.

Salcedo, Erica J. *Information Packet: Latino Youth and the Foster Care System*. National Center for Child Welfare Excellence at the Silberman School of Social Work, 2015.

Villegas, Susy, James Rosenthal, Kirk O'Brien, and Peter J. Pecora. "Educational Outcomes for Adults Formerly in Foster Care: The Role of Ethnicity." *Children and Youth Services Review* 36 (2014): 42–52.

IV. Health

Claiming the Promise of Health and Success for Boys and Men of Color in California. Alliance for Boys and Men of Color, 2015.

Edley, Christopher, and Jorge Ruiz de Velasco, eds. *Changing Places: How Communities Will Improve the Health of Boys of Color.* Berkeley: University of California Press, 2010.

Gallo, Linda C., Frank J. Penedo, Karla Espinosa de los Monteros, and William Argüelles. "Resiliency in the Face of Disadvantage: Do Hispanic Cultural Characteristics Protect Health Outcomes?" *Journal of Personality* 77.6 (2009): 1707–46.

Hough, Richard L., Andrea L. Hazen, Fernando I. Soriano, Patricia Wood, Kristen McCabe, and May Yeh. "Mental Health Care for Latinos: Mental Health Services for Latino Adolescents with Psychiatric Disorders." *Psychiatric Services* 53.12 (2002): 1556–62.

a. Mental Health

Bean, Roy A., and Jason C. Northrup. "Parental Psychological Control, Psychological Autonomy, and Acceptance as Predictors of Self-Esteem in Latino Adolescents." *Journal of Family Issues* 30.11 (2009): 1486–1504.

Gloria, Alberta M., Jeanett Castellanos, Nicholas C. Scull, and Francisco J. Villegas. "Psychological Coping and Well-being of Male Latino Undergraduates: Sobreviviendo la Universidad." *Hispanic Journal of Behavioral Sciences* 31.3 (2009): 317–39.

"Needs of Latino Youth: Part II: Resilience." National Resource Center for Mental Health Promotion and Youth Violence Prevention, 2009.

V. Youth Development

Bandy, Tawana, and Kristin A. Moore. "What Works for Latino/Hispanic Children and Adolescents: Lessons from Experimental Evaluations of Programs and Interventions." *Child Trends* 2011-05 (2011): 1-11.

Berg, Marlene, Emil Coman, and Jean J. Schensul. "Youth Action Research for Prevention: A Multi-Level Intervention Designed to Increase Efficacy and Empowerment Among Urban Youth." *American Journal of Community Psychology* 43.3-4 (2009): 345–59.

Borden, Lynne M., Daniel F. Perkins, Francisco A. Villarruel, Annelise Carleton-Hug, Margaret R. Stone, and Joanne G. Keith. "Challenges and Opportunities to Latino Youth Development Increasing Meaningful Participation in Youth Development Programs." *Hispanic Journal of Behavioral Sciences* 28.2 (2006): 187–208.

Goya, García, Elizabeth Marie Vance, Lacy María Serros, Cheryl Brownstein-Santiago, CBS Consulting Group, and Frontline Solutions. *The Right to Dream: Promising Practices Improve Odds for Latino Men and Boys.* Hispanics in Philanthropy, 2014.

Huerta, Adrian H. "'I Didn't Want My Life to Be Like That': Gangs, College, or the Military for Latino Male High School Students." *Journal of Latino/Latin American Studies* 6.3 (2014): 156–67.

Hurtado, Aída. "Gloria Anzaldúa's Seven Stages of Conocimiento in Redefining Latino Masculinity: José's Story." *Masculinidades y cambio social* 4.1 (2015): 43–84.

"Latino Men and Boys Overview." *The Unity Council*, 2013.

Montero-Sieburth, Martha, and Francisco A. Villarruel, eds. *Making Invisible Latino Adolescents Visible: A Critical Approach to Latino Diversity*, Michigan State University

Series on Children, Youth, and Families, vol. 7. New York: Falmer Press, 2000.

Noguera, Pedro, Aída Hurtado, and Edward Fergus, eds. *Understanding the Disenfranchisement of Latino Men and Boys: Invisible No More*. New York: Routledge, 2012.

Ridings, John W., Lissette M. Piedra, Julio C. Capeles, Raquel Rodríguez, Fernando Freire, and Soo-Jung Byoun. "Building a Latino Youth Program: Using Concept Mapping to Identify Community-Based Strategies for Success." *Journal of Social Service Research* 37.1 (2010): 34–49.

Riggs, Nathaniel R., Amy M. Bohnert, Maria D. Guzman, and Denise Davidson. "Examining the Potential of Community-Based After-School Programs for Latino Youth." *American Journal of Community Psychology* 45.3-4 (2010): 417–29.

VI. Resilience and Critical Pedagogy

Acosta, Curtis. "Pedagogies of Resiliency and Hope in Response to the Criminalization of Latin@ Students." *Journal of Language and Literacy Education* 9.2 (2013): 63–71.

Campa, Blanca. "Critical Resilience, Schooling Processes, and the Academic Success of Mexican Americans in a Community College." *Hispanic Journal of Behavioral Sciences* 32.3 (2010): 429–55.

Kuperminc, Gabriel P., Natalie J. Wilkins, Cathy Roche, and Anabel Álvarez-Jiménez. "Risk, Resilience, and Positive Development Among Latino Youth." In *Handbook of US Latino Psychology: Developmental and Community-Based Perspectives*, edited by Francisco A. Villarruel, Gustavo Carlo, Josefina M. Grau, Margarita Azmitia, Natasha J. Cabrera, and T. Jamie Chahin. Los Angeles: SAGE, 2009. 213–33.

Perez, William, Roberta Espinoza, Karina Ramos, Heidi M. Coronado, and Richard Cortés. "Academic Resilience

Among Undocumented Latino Students." *Hispanic Journal of Behavioral Sciences* 31.2 (2009): 149–81.

Reyes, Jazmin A., and Maurice J. Elias. "Fostering Social-Emotional Resilience Among Latino Youth." *Psychology in the Schools* 48.7 (2011): 723–37.

Rossatto, Cesar A., Cecilia E. Rivas, Daniel B. Heiman, and Juanita Esparza. "'Troublemaking,' 'Making Trouble,' and 'Making It' Through Institutionalized Schooling: Critical Pedagogy as a Transformational Exodus." *Critical Education* 6.5 (2015): 1–33.

CHAPTER 2

Profiles in Best Practice: The Healing and Transformation of Latino Men and Boys

Frank de Jesús Acosta

The purpose of this publication is to advance best practice in policy making and programming related to at-risk Latino men and boys. In this context, "best practice" is understood to mean supporting culturally based, comprehensive prevention and intervention models with a demonstrated history of efficacy in addressing the complex, deeply rooted disparities endangering the individual, familial and communal bonds that are most vital to these young men. Through work that advances best practice in this space, especially work building on the untapped cultural capital and latent intellectual capacity that resides in Latino men and boys, we can dramatically expand these young people's overall life prospects for success in American society and economy.

Overcoming Disparity focuses on two leading program models and visionary leaders that advance best practice in their engagement of Latino men and boys in the Southwestern United States, using restorative justice principles and modalities: (1) the California-based National Compadres Network (NCN)/National Latino Fatherhood and Family Institute (NLFFI), guided by Jerry Tello, and (2) the New Mexico-based La Plazita (Little Center) Institute, guided by Albino García, Jr.

It should be noted that our past research and present investigation have alerted us to the important work of numerous other organizations, networks and projects located in California that effectively utilize culturally based practices and allied community innovations to better serve at-risk Latino men and boys. These entities include, among others: Santa Cruz Barrios Unidos, Communities United for Restorative Youth Justice (CURYJ), Homies Unidos and Homeboy Industries. In fact, while we are unable to profile these exemplary organizational models in this publication, the essential work of each of these field leaders will be centrally featured in future "Best Practice Profiles" to be posted online at artepublicopress.com as well as the Insight Center for Community Economic Development's corporate website at insightcced.org/latino.young.men.boys/.

A unifying core element of the best practice models that are the primary subject of this volume is that their guiding values, principles and strategies are deeply rooted in and/or significantly informed by the philosophy of La Cultura Cura, or "the Healing Culture." They all use indigenous and time-tested Latino traditions, symbols and rituals as central elements of their effective efforts to rebuild lives and communities that are otherwise at risk. They invoke a strong sense of community pride and purpose in the young people they serve. And they involve particularized engagements in education, training and community activism that are intended to advance real democracy and opportunity in low-income, grassroots Latino communities.

It is our informed opinion, along with that of our panel of advisors, that cultural fluency and respect must be the cornerstones of any discipline or model that can be legitimately designated as a best practice in this space. Research and lived experience reveal that where gang- and violence-involved Latino men and boys are concerned, only healing, transformation and purposeful living can serve as lasting ingredients for ultimate redemption and life success. In this regard, the La Cultura Cura philosophy and framework embody the fundamental tenets of best practice across disciplines, practices, systems and policy platforms. To provide a working description and framework of La Cultura Cura for the presentation of the profiles to follow, we offer the following language developed by one of our subjects, Jerry Tello, who is a leading pioneer in the field:

> La Cultura Cura, or "Cultural Based Healing," is a path to healing and healthy development which is inextricably linked to restoring one's true cultural identity as the foundation of well-being for individuals, families, communities and society alike. This is achieved through a generational process of learning and/or remembering one's true cultural values, principles, customs and traditions. La Cultural Cura integrates healing-informed approaches to education, engagement, service delivery and aftercare as a vital first step in reducing life-threatening outcomes for Latino and Native boys. To promulgate La Cultura Cura at the systems and institutional levels, what is needed is a framework that provides culturally based programming, network and capacity-building and systems transformation. Culturally based innovation and capacity currently exist and require replication to fully inform and prevent disparity impacting Latino boys and men.[1]

A primary goal of *Overcoming Disparity* is to present descriptive statements and profiles of field leaders along these lines, assembled directly from interviews, as well as from their

---

[1]Jerry Tello telephone Interview, by Frank de Jesús Acosta, July 7, 2015.

various records and archives. The publication is also intended to place on the public record important allied content that is potentially valuable to field practitioners, such as training and educational curricula, program plans, logic models and impact evaluation materials. While pursuing these aims, we also present a narrative report on each featured group's essential approach to the work and their respective successes in the field, based on interviews with the leadership of each profiled organization. Together, these elements of our reporting herein seek to capture the dynamic breadth of leading work in the national Latino youth and community development space and the common best practices field leaders employ to optimize their intended contributions to Latino men and boys.

Our informing interviews were shaped by common "guiding questions," which consisted of the following.

Guiding Questions

1. Speak to why American society should/must better understand and respond to the social and economic disparities faced by Latino boys and young men. Why is it critical for the nation to address the dire circumstances and promote the healthy development of this population?

2. The book series highlights best practice models that are self-identified as culturally based and rooted in what they call "La Cultura Cura." What core values and principles must guide policy, strategies, practices, programs and services that would constitute comprehensive, integrated community frameworks for best practice rooted in cultural competency? What is the evidence that these La Cultura Cura best practice strategies actually work?

Please cite from the list below good examples that amplify and illustrate ongoing innovations, learning and evidence-based successes from your work in California and elsewhere, nationally, across essential arenas.

• youth development, culturally based rites of passage
• violence prevention
• gang and delinquency intervention
• restorative juvenile justice strategies (e.g., corrective, remedial, conciliatory versus punitive)
• restorative criminal justice strategies (e.g., corrective, remedial, conciliatory versus punitive)
• healthy community development

3. What are key challenges, opportunities and priorities for the Latino men and boys (LMB) and boys and men of color (BMoC) fields in California and nationwide? Please cite examples that pertain to your specific community, programs, systems and foundation partners. For example:

• The California Endowment's Building Healthy Communities
• Sierra Health Foundation's Positive Youth Justice initiative
• W. K. Kellogg Foundation's investment in boys and young men of color
• California Alliance for Boys and Men of Color
• Alameda County Coalition for Criminal Justice Reform
• Dignity in Schools Campaign
• My Brother's Keeper Initiative
• Gathering for Justice

Note: While the White House-supported My Brothers' Keeper Initiative primarily focuses on the "school-to-prison pipeline," mostly addressing the need for reforms in juvenile justice and education systems, critical additional disparities that must be addressed for BMoC in communities across the country include:

• intergenerational poverty and trauma
• poor educational advancement
• discriminatory justice practices (law enforcement, adjudication, sentencing)
• disproportionate incarceration and punishment-oriented corrections
• exposure to violence, gangs, firearm injury and death
• training, jobs and economic advancement

The collective experience of the *Overcoming Disparity*'s principal editors, contributors and advisors represents over five decades of interdisciplinary learning and leadership, social change activism and culturally rooted community-based work with at-risk youth in Latino and other communities of color. While there is thus no lack of seasoned leadership perspective in this domain, there is nevertheless real need for enhanced intellectual documentation and framing of the issues and opportunities associated with the nation's large and fast-growing population of young Latino males. The pages that follow seek to address that imperative.

CHAPTER 3

Jerry Tello, National Compadres Network

Interview by Frank de Jesús Acosta

I first became aware of the groundbreaking culturally based work of Jerry Tello during my tenure as the senior program officer overseeing the California Wellness Foundation's Violence Prevention Initiative in 1996. Over the past twenty years, I have witnessed firsthand how Tello has utilized his expertise in applying La Cultura Cura in the areas of fatherhood, family strengthening, community peace, healing and culturally based violence prevention/intervention. For some thirty years, Jerry Tello has dedicated his life to preventing and healing the pain of relationship/community violence, teen pregnancy, father-lessness and internalized oppression. As co-founder of the National Compadres Network (established in 1988) with Executive Director Héctor Sánchez-Flores, Jerry has provided teaching presentations to more than a half million people, trained more than a thousand facilitators in culturally based curricula and mentored hundreds of grassroots youth and community development practitioners. He has authored various curricula addressing issues of fatherhood, male rites of passage, relationship and gang violence prevention, teen pregnancy prevention, family strengthening and community peace.

The core of NCN's work is Círculo based (an established sacred space for communal gathering). The approach involves a circle of community and life in which special terms of engagement apply to identify and resolve issues, surface opportunities for growth and celebrate victories and advancements. Whole organizations of practitioners and facilitators have begun to evolve from this practice of collective growth and exchange over recent years. Efforts focused on multiple issue areas and community needs are being advanced in Círculos all across the country that base their work on these teachings and frameworks.

Of the many available curricula addressing the particular circumstances of men and boys of color, the National Compadre Network's El Joven Noble (the Noble Young Man) program is the only sanctioned evidence-based Chicano/Latino curriculum in the nation. El Joven Noble is a comprehensive, indigenous-based youth leadership development program that supports and guides young men through a rigorous rites of passage process while focusing on the prevention of substance abuse, teen pregnancy, relationship violence, gang violence and school failure.

To begin our interview, I asked Jerry, **"Why should American society invest in better understanding and responses to the social and economic disparities faced by Latino boys and young men?"**

Jerry prefaces his response to my question by acknowledging that he has been honored to be a messenger and translator of the teachings of our ancestors and feels blessed to have been guided by indigenous Mexicano, Chicano and Native elders of the tradition. He stresses that the impetus of NCN's work was informed by a group of Chicano, Native men who established an Hombres Círculo (Men's Circle). The men gathered in prayer and dialogue to recapture the true spirit of El Hombre Noble and to take personal responsibility to help advance healing and community stewardship over the coming seven generations (a traditional indigenous marker of contemporary society's responsibilities to future ages).

Tello goes on to point up a fundamental issue facing people residing in the United States who are of Latino descent, namely, that Latinos have been largely invisible in this country throughout time immemorial and remain so. "Historically," he says, "we are not seen or considered. If anything, we are only factored or considered in relation to the welfare of others—not as valued or respected human beings worthy of being considered as equals." As Tello sees it, "Our worth is measured in relation to white privileged populations or in comparison to the distress of African American populations—as if we don't matter in and of ourselves." He concludes by asserting that "this is the crux of the issue."

Tello believes the longstanding reality of Latino invisibility in America, informed by a legacy of racially biased leaders, systems and world views, demonstrates a complete human disregard in the face of our present population numbers and ancestral presence in California and other important states. On the practical side, he points out that Latinos are now the majority population in California and represent numerically significant portions of many local communities and regions nationally. Nevertheless, because current census reporting practices and priorities often fail to fully capture the growth, needs and still-untapped potential of Latino populations across the land, Tello and other Latino community leaders are critical of government population data and systems and of the policies they inform. According to Tello, "They try to appease us by doing language translation, adaptation or adding us to the data and conversation as an addendum; but it is merely a perfunctory effort, because it never really honors who we are or authentically embraces the multilayered and multigenerational issues that we face."

Ancestral Roots of Latinos in the United States

According to Tello, "The irony is that in California and many areas of the Southwest, these are our ancestral lands." As he reflects upon it, "The spirit of our people lives here. Our people work the fields that feed the nation and the world—others are eating food that we plant, cultivate, pick, package and even prepare. Our blood, sweat and earthly remains are in the soil that feeds the nation; our spirit and that of our ancestors is alive within everyone who partakes of the harvests of this land."

Tello warns that Latino people must never relegate themselves to being mere fodder and fuel for an economic system that does not treat them with appropriate dignity, fairness and equity for their many contributions to national wealth building. Indeed, he believes that from a systemic and spiritual point of view, mainstream American society suffers greatly from its failure to embrace Latinos, who, as Tello sees it, provide vital teachings, traditions, values and history that can both inform and transform the nation and our world. He believes the indigenous Latino world view can bring the planet to a place of needed healing and sacred interconnectedness.

Specifically, as Tello sees it, Latinos offer the world a perspective that is rooted in the universal sacredness and connectedness of everyone. As such, they have a special duty and responsibility to serve as agents of needed social change. Latino citizens and residents of the United States are primarily people of indigenous/Native descent (having their ancestral roots in what is now the "American" Southwest, Mexico, and Central and South America). They share a history over the centuries that defines them as communal, relationship-centered people. And their notions of relationship are about connecting not only with other human beings but also with all creation: the earth, sun, water and wind—all the sacred elements of the universe. It is this world view, Tello contends, rich with life-affirming guiding values and accumulated wisdoms, that has much to offer our increasingly broken world, a world that is sadly being destroyed by an artificial culture of greed, mass consumption, racial chauvinism and a politics of privilege.

Medicine in Our Culture

Tello draws on the ancient ancestral belief that the world has entered into the time of the Quinto Sol (Fifth Sun), a time of profound transition and change. He explains that counter to designations by Western mainstream anthropologists that Latinos are a male-dominant culture, in fact Spanish-speaking Americans are actually matrilineal people, which means female or mother centered. While historical developments and forced acculturation may have begun to alter this cornerstone of Latino culture during recent decades, prophecy says that Latinos must return to their indigenous ways in order to help reground people in the wisdom of our grandmothers, to once again become a matrilineal society. "What the grandmothers, elders, medicine people all tells us," Tello says, "is that we must return to the world view that we are all sacred. This is vitally important to Latino men and boys, because in the present distorted cultural paradigm, they see themselves as not wanted, but rather as the problem, the delinquent, unvalued and easily dispensable. How can a truly loving society so easily justify kicking these young men out of school, locking them up, medicating or deporting them? This mirrors the worst treatment of unwanted pets."

In addition, Tello reflects, Western thought tells us that we are all born a blank slate, therefore needing to be taught or socialized, indoctrinated or assimilated into this world. But according to our ancestral world view, Tello states, "all children are born sacred, with ancestral wisdom, ancestral medicine, blessing and spirit. Unfortunately, the young ones born today are also born with intergenerational pain, trauma and wounds. They inherit both sides as part of their spiritual DNA." In this sense, says Tello, our children are a sacred medicine all their own. In their healing and transformation is the healing and transformation of everyone. We express to all people in this country that it is a collective first responsibility of everyone to welcome all children and to create a safe space for them, an environment in which they can learn and grow to fulfill their sacred purpose as a benefit to the world.

Why La Cultura Cura?

Tello believes that culture is the lifeblood of all people's well-being. For Latinos, this inherited *cultura*—both intuitive and that which has been passed on through ancient writings, stories, traditions, rites of passage and ceremony—is the anchor to their authentic world view. It is the source of their highest humanity, innate wisdom, imagination, medicine, identity and spirit. The life-affirming tenets of La Cultura Cura are:

- We are all sacred.
- Everyone has a sacred purpose.
- Everyone has ancestral wisdom, values and traditions that are the basis for one's lifelong rites of passage.
- Everyone needs elders, teachers and community to guide them and provide a safe place to heal, learn and grow.

The world view engendered and promulgated by this philosophy is inherently focused on the well-being and betterment of all relations.

Tello believes the concept of La Cultura Cura is ancient and has been written about and taught by many others over the ages. First and foremost, these are principles for living. He identifies and embraces his sacred purpose and responsibility to take the concepts and teachings of La Cultura Cura and operationalize them, filtering them so that they can be taught correctly and understood in today's pluralistic society in a way that is useful in everyday life. This has been his life's work for the last forty years; it is what brought him and Héctor Sánchez together to establish the National Compadres Network.

Through the work of the network, Tello, Sánchez and their colleagues have made this their mission: bringing these asset-based practices of ancestral teachings and medicine into today's communities and society. Their intent is to carry on the teachings of the ancestors and to heal the present generation's pain of oppression by bringing forth a spirit of renewed cultural identity and purpose to overcome present circumstances and create a better world. In effect, they seek to spread the medicine that enables the creation of caring environments in which the well-being of all relations matter equally.

Latinos Represent an Intercultural Nexus

Tloque Nahuaque is the concept of sacred interconnectedness. Tello explains that among Latinos presently living in the United States, nearly 85 percent have Native blood or DNA from pre-Conquest Mexico, Central and South America, passed on from their mothers. As legacies of a long history of indigenous civilization and struggle in the New World, they hold certain teachings and medicine that they bring to the whole of humanity. These assets represent a confluence of diverse cultures and elements from every direction, as well as unifying characteristics that invoke collective healing, wholeness and harmony across the planet.

Jerry Tello asserts that Latino and indigenous people across the Americas carry the Mayan concept of *In Lak'ech Hala Ken,* meaning, "I am the other you, and you are the other me." This is the belief and life tenet that we are all connected; when one person or community is wounded, we are all wounded. Similarly, when one heals or thrives, everyone heals and thrives. This world view of interconnectedness fundamentally counters the influences of individualism, indifference and hatred that increasingly challenge modern Western social cohesion. It opposes the forces that bring oppression, whereby certain sectors hoard resources and arbitrarily create a society of race-based meritocracy (enforced by violent control) so they can live in privilege at the detrimental expense of others.

Tello warns that America needs to realize that Latinos (and especially younger members of our communities) are increasingly the backbone of the American workforce and consumer economy. He observes, for example, that the viability of the US Social Security system is ultimately dependent on their economic success and well-being. With continued neglect and marginalization of Latino boys and men, the nation suffers. Yet present systems and policies fail to educate, employ and empower Latinos, thus neutralizing their natural ingenuity and enterprise. In this way, current systems and policies jeopardize the nation's future prospects for creating a more sustainable economy and more democratically responsive institutions.

It is incumbent on the society to enable Latinos to use their cultural medicine to heal and restore themselves and to benefit the broader society. If America fails to acknowledge and cultivate Latinos' human potential to help advance civil society, economics, science, industry, agriculture, medicine, education and the arts, our collective future as a nation will be fundamentally jeopardized. For these reasons, says Tello, disregarding or suppressing Latino culture is ultimately self-defeating for America.

The best practice models profiled in the book series are all self-identified as culturally based and rooted in what they call "La Cultura Cura." What is the evidence that La Cultura Cura best practice strategies actually work?

In reply to this question, Tello reiterates that it is critical for mainstream America to recognize that within Latino culture exists the medicine to heal and change the dysfunctions in our barrios and the larger society alike. He argues that where culture is truly manifest, there is no place for gangs, interpersonal and domestic violence, substance abuse, child abuse, elder abuse and neglect. Where La Cultura Cura lives, says Tello, there are inherent checks and balances on all of these social ills.

The challenge and the opportunity is to create space for the basic principles of La Cultura Cura to operate against the backdrop of so much historical and contemporary resistance. Tello reminds me in our exchange about the experience of cultural genocide in this country, which has directly caused intergenerational trauma and wounded Latinos and other significant minority population groups. This legacy of violence and cultural-economic dominance in turn has severely diminished the protective factors, or checks and balances, in contemporary Latino individuals, families and communities that would otherwise bolster their condition. The culturally erosive environment is compounded by what Tello calls "a country, society and world that is losing its spirit." What La Cultura Cura tries to do is reinoculate individuals, families, communities and systems to the ancestral past and medicine that are ultimately the source of their personal and societal empowerment.

Natural Opportunity Factors

Tello reminds me as we move through our interview that La Cultura Cura focuses on natural opportunity factors—in essence, nurturing what is inherently healthy within individuals, families and communities. It is here that the concept of *Tloque Nahuaque*, or interconnected sacredness, relates to the collective wholeness of all. Tello and his colleagues engaged in advancing the NCN approach are mindful that every culture bestows important blessings upon its people; wherever we sit in the world, each person carries the necessary powers to create life-affirming environments. Similarly, Tello observes, we all can learn from the darkness and the shadows. Ailments and struggle are naturally neither good nor bad; they are simply fodder (or medicine) for learning and growth. Given these factors, the NCN model of youth and community development builds not only on preordained, standard curricular content but also and even more importantly on the lived experience of Latino youth and families in ways that draw on their natural cycles of life and gainful pursuit.

Lessons from Soledad Prison

Jerry recalled him and Nane Alejandrez of Santa Cruz Barrios Unidos talking with a particular group of inmates at one of the correctional facilities they visited together after an honoring, blessing ceremony. These men received a presentation stressing the importance of them being present in the lives of their children and families as fathers and grandfathers (i.e., instruction in La Cultura Cura's Five Valors and El Hombre Noble—"the Noble Man"). Despite the clear benefits of these learnings, many of the inmates still expressed simultaneous distress and sadness over their circumstances, a feeling that despite having much to offer following their newfound growth and transformation, they could not adequately contribute to their families back home because of their incarcerated status and physical dislocation. Several who had children voiced particular disillusionment that from prison they could not be good fathers.

Tello tells me he reminded these men (most of them young adults) that they still have power and prerogative, even in their current conditions of forced detention. There were many things, he told them, that they could do to remain connected and useful to their families, communities and the larger society. For example, they could pray for their family members, loved ones and friends. They could write them to express their love and make it a priority to stay current on their life interests, successes and struggles, demonstrating that they care. They could also maintain a spiritual and conscious presence in society, despite their physical separation from life outside of prison, by staying informed and recording and sharing their views about life, love and society. Tello tells me he advised these young men to keep journals with daily entries, including prayers, thoughts, hopes and memories. He also urged them to share the lessons of their imprisonment with others around them, both inside and outside of prison.

As it turns out, personal voice is one of the most vital currencies that the La Cultura Cura approach seeks to bring forward in the young people it serves. Voice in this context can be reflected through both written and spoken word, as well as in visual imagery via various forms of artistic expression.

Dignity, the First Valor of La Cultura Cura

As we progress through our interview, Tello shares with me how his experience working with incarcerated men and boys has taught him the true power of *cultura* as a means of removing disabling shackles from at-risk people and youth, despite their circumstances. Eliminating or at least productively managing shame is foremost among Tello's concerns. The presence of injury or personal failure, as he sees it, does not absolve one of the responsibility of reckoning, nor does it annul one's inherent sacredness. There is infinite healing and transformative power in love, forgiveness and atonement (i.e., transformative justice), according to Tello. The ancestral medicine of La Cultura Cura is ultimately liberating, empowering and already in our people's DNA. Dignity and sacredness, says Tello, are there within people to claim regardless of circumstance, and they are ready to be activated. In the teachings of La Cultura Cura, self-help plays an essential role. According to those teachings, Tello reminds me, finding the courage to reclaim personal dignity, the will to change, heal and transform and the inclination to embrace one's sacred purpose must come from within each individual.

Respect, the Second Valor of La Cultura Cura

Tello especially emphasizes that to be whole, individuals must respect their historical ancestral vision. In his view, no one was created to do harm to oneself, others or their community. In fact, he says, people are born with the responsibility of living in a way that affirms life. At birth, people carry the innate spirit or ability to *respond* to life, which does not always offer a friendly or nurturing environment. La Cultura Cura helps people of indigenous origins to better understand the roots of their pain, imperfections and dysfunctions. This understanding in turn brings revelation that the negative manifestation of self in an imperfect world is neither a necessary nor a desirable state of being. Only the revelation of true self and purpose, says Tello, can enable Latino men and boys to reflect, learn, dream and rediscover their authentic, sacred selves. This in turn enables them both to become more worthy of respect and to act more effectively as instruments of respect in the broader society.

Confianza Interconnectedness, the Third Valor of La Cultura Cura

At this point, Jerry reminds me of the living principles of *In Lak'ech Hala Ken* and *Tloque Nahuaque*. This world view tells us that, in essence, healing and restoration is not an individual, but familial, communal and social proposition—transformation is for the collective. Building on these concepts, Tello tells me that the healing and transformation of those living wounded and in brokenness create new light and energy, a new reality. In its essence, he says, the journey informed by La Cultura Cura requires appreciation that one does not operate in a disconnected vacuum from the rest of society. Rather, the practice of La Cultura Cura demands trust and inherently lends a more connected view of life and a corresponding sense of social responsibility. In this regard, says Tello, a former inmate or criminal offender who is healed and transformed in the loving medicine of La Cultura Cura (including owning personal responsibility for doing harm to others and reckoning wrongs) is an essential element of creating a better world based on shared connectivity and responsibility rather than interpersonal conflict and intergroup violence.

Cariño, Movement on Unconditional Love or Olin, the Fourth Valor of La Cultura Cura

Jerry Tello is passionate about the concept of movement towards life-affirming growth, a process that he sees as being ultimately rooted in love and caring. An aspect of everyone's sacred purpose, he says, is bridging one's sacredness, dignity, respect and connectedness to self, family and the community of one's own people. Absent these footprints, he asserts, it is impossible to meaningfully care for or embrace others further away from one's personal circle of experience and relations. In order to strengthen our collective capacities to care for one another in the pursuit of a more harmonious social reality, says Tello, we need to build constructive pathways that facilitate healthy choices and responsible living. In effect, says Tello, for many Latino men and boys, the pathways to living in this way have been seriously damaged and corrupted in contemporary society by the evolution of distorted values, systems and institutions that promote hyperindividualism, inequality and privilege.

Spirituality, the Fifth Valor of La Cultura Cura

According to Tello, the time has come to reestablish *Ixtli* and *Yollotl*, the Nahuatl words for "face" and "heart." La Cultura Cura focuses on living life with a frontal sense of spirit, *ganas* (will) and harmony in relation to others and all creation. Tello says getting to this state of living requires learning to talk, walk and live in sacredness. It requires impeccable personal conduct and relations across all aspects and realms of life. It requires creating a social order that more broadly ensures this type of nurturing environment and, in turn, demands that systems and institutions must be willing to change and facilitate the introduction of more culturally unifying principles, values and practices in the public domain.

Culture: Transforming Systems and Institutions

Tello is very clear that for La Cultura Cura to become a truly transformative force for Latino men and boys, for community and society, there needs to be a fundamental cultural shift in the policies and practices of public and private systems and institutions that influence or otherwise greatly determine people's quality of life. For this to happen, Tello stresses, the core values and principles of La Cultura Cura must be more broadly recognized as legitimate and valuable developmental, prevention and intervention tools. He also posits that the effective application of La Cultura Cura in community and institutional settings must be more broadly embraced by policy leaders, researchers and social investors of all types as proven evidence-based practice.

An essential critique that Tello and many other Latino youth and community development leaders have expressed over the years is that the black/white paradigm traditionally used to examine everything "race related" in America must be expanded. Indeed, Tello argues, the growing national dialogue regarding disparities faced by men and boys of color calls for fast-growing Latino populations and their foremost leaders to advance a more robust and representative voice on the issues. The groundwork for this to occur has been laid by the National Compadres Network over the past thirty years through the training of thousands of interdisciplinary leaders and practitioners in La Cultura Cura principles, practices and models.

Building on this history and capacity, NCN has worked during recent years to make inroads with thousands of education and community health professionals, through training sessions that infuse the cultural principles that are central to its core mission. In this work, NCN has focused on developing not only the intellect and skills of young Latinos, but also their character, self-worth and nurturing spirits. This is the essence of restorative justice. In working with mental health professionals, NCN stresses the cultural principle that healing requires not only mental but also emotional and spiritual well-being. By the same token, working with Latino men and boys involved in the California criminal and juvenile justice systems informs NCN advocacy efforts to encourage a moving away from punitive and fear-based methodologies and toward a more transformative model focused on healing and restorative justice.

An important cadre of the La Cultura Cura network is made up of interdisciplinary practitioners, organizers and leaders from the community-based nonprofit organization sector that principally serves Latino men and boys. These professionals and paraprofessionals represent many diverse fields, systems and program interests, including, among others, family support services; health, mental health and social services; alternative schools; foster care; substance abuse treatment programs; and community development entities. But primarily they involve a broad and growing spectrum of youth development, prevention, intervention and reentry organizations and networks focused on such issues as violence prevention, gang intervention and restorative juvenile and criminal justice.

Among the anchor organizations operating in the field that have been close collaborative partners of NCN over the years, and that have thus applied some or all of its teachings, are American Indians in Texas (AIT), San Antonio; Fathers and Families of San Joaquin; CURYJ, Oakland; Motivating Individual Leadership for Public Advancement (MILPA), Salinas; Teatro Izcalli, San Diego; Gang Rescue and Support Project (GRASP), Denver, Colorado; and Montgomery County Department of Health and Human Services, Maryland. These groups have worked with NCN over the years to learn the core philosophy, principles, values and practices of La Cultura Cura. In fact, all of the organizations we have identified as best practice models across California and the Southwest work in collaboration in one form or another and have had some of their leadership, staff, volunteers and/or service populations trained by NCN in one or more of its various La Cultura Cura training sessions.

Building a Legitimate Field of Inquiry

Jerry Tello has spent the last forty years (and thirty years alone with NCN) developing, teaching, testing, applying, learning, innovating and concretizing the La Cultura Cura model, manifesting its application across multiple disciplines. His core aim has been to help operationalize the model's philosophy, values, principles and practices into an accessible and applicable body of knowledge for everyday life and diverse fields, disciplines, systems and policies. In the process, NCN has sought to create a model framework that is conceptually understandable for multiple cross-cultural audiences in communities and systems—touching in each instance the individual, family, community, intercommunity, social, civic, economic and ecological realms. Under Tello's abiding leadership, moreover, NCN has sought to develop a model that can be measured and broadly recognized as evidence based.

Evidence of Efficacy

In addition to providing a broad array of organizational and program evaluations and special reports on regional issues affecting agricultural populations of our state, NCN has worked intensively for some thirty years in Central California. Tello tells me during our interview that the network has surfaced some especially promising initiatives in rural central California. The most recent efforts among these have been in the cities and surrounding communities served by the Central Valley schools. These efforts are of special interest to this publication because they have activated the full array of NCN's model and tool kit—spurring in the process important innovations in the application of La Cultura Cura that have helped to expand knowledge about cross-cultural proficiency in practice, systems and policy for Latino men and boys in education, justice and other important sectors that impact the quality of life and opportunities in multicultural communities.

The work in the Central Valley grew out of a partnership with California's leading health philanthropy, the California Endowment, and the Central California Children's Institute. The institute invited NCN to a regional meeting of educators to address the disproportionate suspension and expulsion of young Latinos and other men and boys of color at area schools. This led to NCN being invited to provide a series of presentations and training sessions across the region for schools that wanted to improve the educational participation and outcomes of Latino men and boys. The leadership of the district had come to terms with the demographic realities of a majority Latino community and school population, realizing it needed to address its failing performance and make changes. Today, as a result, local schools across the region have formalized partnerships with NCN and allied groups that are helping to gradually improve rates of school attendance and success for young latino men by lessening their engagement with drugs and alcohol, unwanted pregnancy, violence and local law enforcement.

Central Valley, California

According to Tello, the Central Valley School District (CVSD) has contracted NCN to provide La Cultura Cura training in twenty-three schools for a total of 2,300 staff members, including principals, administrators, teachers, counselors, nurses, health and mental health workers, coaches, clerical staff, parents and students. The districts and individual schools are trying to address the disparities facing not only Latino students but also disenfranchised African American student populations. Tello tells me that NCN finds in many educational institutions a recurrent situation for students of color wherein they are being systematically identified as having behavioral problems. The inevitable result is that these students (and especially male students) of color are highly overrepresented in school suspension, expulsion, underperformance and early dropout.

Building School and Community Capacity

NCN is working with the CVSD to advance the philosophy and practice of transformational learning, healing, justice and leadership as a package of connected concepts and strategies. These interconnected strategies work to help students feel valued, wanted, welcomed and safe. They infuse essential culturally based values and practices into the educational process in ways that help to create an improved climate for learning and growth.

To accomplish all of this, NCN is providing multitiered mass training sessions for up to one hundred individuals at a time, focusing on the philosophical underpinnings of La Cultura Cura. These large-scale sessions are followed up in turn with smaller site-by-site training sessions at individual schools in order to build their cultural fluency and integration of related community values, principles and practices throughout the entire educational process.

Transformative Justice in Central Valley Schools

In the next stage of our exchange, Tello turns his attention to specific aspects of the National Compadres Network's work in the Central Valley schools. He starts by identifying important stakeholder touch points for Latino men and boys, beginning with the systems personnel and leadership, teachers and students who are involved in this work and are central to its advancement. But he also tells me about the vital role of the parents, families and neighborhoods that surround young at-risk, gang-involved Latinos, supporting and encouraging them as circle keepers to pursue a path of redemption and recovery. NCN works extensively with educators to promote their understanding of the critical role schools play in establishing (or prohibiting) a comprehensive transformative justice infra-structure in low-income Latino communities. Some of the schools that NCN is engaged with have begun to implement transformational justice practice curricula, including the inte-gration of healing and support circles (Círculos) in classrooms and on campus.

Progress Toward Change

According to Tello, the district-wide infusion of La Cul-tura Cura modalities in Central Valley schools has started to change the narrative; that is, cross-cultural concepts and lan-guage find their way into education-related institutional dis-course and practice. As we advance our interview, he proudly shares with me that he recently saw a poster on one of the local school's walls. It prominently featured the La Cultura Cura principles:

- Our children are sacred and should be welcomed to the world as they are.
- Our children have a sacred purpose, and it is our respon-sibility to nurture this calling.
- Our children come with ancient teachings of their cul-ture that must be acknowledged and recognized, along with Western teachings.
- Our children deserve a secure and safe place in which to learn, heal, grow and give back to society.

NCN is now engaged in a multiyear partnership with the Central Valley schools to develop e-courses intended to enhance teachers' cultural proficiency and responsiveness to the needs of their students, and especially their male Latino students. E-course topics will include, among other things, creating a healthy school climate; creating a positive, culturally based classroom environment; dealing with student problems from a healing-informed versus a punitive perspective; and developing teaching plans that more fully account for the social, political and economic realities facing multicultural children in contemporary America. The district will engage in a substantive evaluation and reflection of its present philosophy and practice in this area, to further align wherever possible with the La Cultura Cura framework.

Salinas, California

Tello reminds me that he and NCN now have a thirty-year track record working with grassroots leaders and organizations all across California and the nation. In fact, just in California, over the past decade NCN has worked extensively in Salinas, Monterey County, San Benito, Watsonville and Gilroy, among other places. More than 140 La Cultura Cura practitioners have been formally trained, including social workers, mental health professionals, teachers, gang workers, probation and juvenile justice staff, recreation workers, library staff, community activists, parents and local residents.

A growing array of people representing many diverse professional disciplines, fields, systems and segments of society are thus now trained in La Cultura Cura philosophy across various NCN curricular touch points, including its Joven Noble (Noble Young Man), Cara y Corazón (Face and Heart) and Xinachtli (Seed) training and engagement programs. Tello explains to me that it is a deliberate strategy of NCN to produce community advocates who can effectively join forces with others to challenge how local systems treat men and boys of color. To do so, NCN purposefully encourages those formally trained in La Cultura Cura to share their work and to collaborate whenever and wherever possible.

NCN next–stage strategy is to build an even larger base of La Cultura Cura–proficient practitioners. The aim of this work, however, is to build community, not simply a network of practitioners, organizers and service providers. In this vein, NCN utilizes various elements of the *Cultura* tapestry to unify its followers in common language and purpose, exposing them to ceremony, *curanderos* (traditional healers), medicine people, storytellers, practitioners versed in treating posttraumatic stress disorder, and health researchers and professionals who seek to treat socioneurological issues. All this is done with the central goal in mind of moving the paradigm from one that sees young people as bad or as a social ill to one that sees them as wounded but still full of potential.

In Salinas, NCN's efforts in these areas have been especially pronounced. The following paragraphs provide brief highlights of what some of this work entails.

Círculos, a Critical Infrastructure

The creation and support of multifocused Círculos (peer group circles focused, for example, on issues of healing; community peace, justice and mediation; and intergenerational and intergroup exchange) is critical to making La Cultura Cura an organic and relevant practice in all facets of community life. Círculos provide the recognized legitimate space in which to gather human and systems resources for the purpose of healing (both of self and others), building community and promoting the well-being of all. Ultimately, these Círculos become safe communal spaces from which to support Latinos and other men and boys of color who are trying to heal and change. These include gang members, prison inmates, people on probation, recovering addicts and alcoholics and young single fathers trying to make their way. It is also where everyday community residents go to reroot in *cultura* or share in uplifting intercultural exchange, learning, healing and celebration.

The effective use of Círculos has been especially prevalent in and around Salinas, particularly in the context of helping communities and loved ones cope with losses from gang death and violence and associated criminal detentions implicating Latino men and boys.

Círculos, Places of Healing

According to Jerry Tello, Círculos have been created in Salinas, as elsewhere, largely for grieving, especially where there has been a heightened level of violence and recent related killings. In 2014, he says, a spate of four officer-involved shootings of Latino men generated widespread anger and pain within Salinas's Spanish-speaking community. According to Tello, Círculos and the presence of seasoned Circle Keepers kept the healing philosophy of La Cultura Cura front and center in ways that helped those most directly implicated (such as affected family members and surviving gunshot victims and witnesses) to resist the impulse to support additional violence in retaliation.

The Salinas Círculo thus helped to channel energy that could have easily manifested itself in further destruction and instead turned that energy into collective healing and positive, life-affirming community engagement. Indeed, the Salinas Círculo has become the recognized dedicated space from which all elements of the affected community can constructively address

law enforcement issues, community dispute resolution needs
and crisis interventions affecting the entire region.

Salinas, Springboard for Racial Equity and Healing

Jerry reports to me that NCN's ongoing work in Salinas
has served as a springboard for very promising racial equity and
healing work across the city's multiple population groups.
With funding support from the California Endowment, NCN
recently partnered with Race Forward, a multimedia racial justice organization, to codevelop an initiative intended to
address racial equity and healing in Salinas.

Tello goes on to tell me the City of Salinas has committed to participate in this work by undertaking a comprehensive review that will enable it to assess possible improvements
and reforms in local policy, procedure and practice across the
jurisdiction's various departments—this with an eye to
improving racial equity in all aspects of local governance.
Accordingly, NCN and Race Forward have conducted training sessions on the issues with the top administrative staff
from every department in the city, including the local police
and fire departments, the city planner's office, the city's health
and mental health agencies, the various court and probation
authorities and the Salinas Public Library.

As a major aspect of this cutting-edge work, NCN and
Race Forward engaged Salinas systems leaders in a reflection
and discovery process intended to increase their understanding of trauma and healing from a La Cultura Cura perspective.
They examined issues of race and oppression, discrimination
and unconscious bias that have found their way into the daily
practice of city agencies and offices. This, Tello explains to
me, has led to the development of an evaluative and planning
framework to allow systems leaders and decision makers to see

their community differently, in ways that can help them to better understand and prioritize issues.

Tello goes on to alert me that NCN and Race Forward also convened fifty nongovernmental community leadership representatives and trained them on the issues through the same process. The two groups were then convened together. What resulted, says Jerry, was essentially a large Círculo focused on racial healing and equity. A combined leadership group was formed and charged with developing a strategic plan to help the City of Salinas achieve greater racial equity, guided by the La Cultura Cura framework and principles. NCN will now work individually with various city departments to provide ongoing support to leadership and rank-and-file staff on how to apply La Cultura Cura principles, to develop more responsive and appropriate policies and practices.

The end goal of this work, according to Jerry, is to create a common narrative around race, discrimination, privilege, oppression, wounds and healing that can ultimately produce a safer and more harmonious civic culture in and around Salinas. While this is a long-term process, to be sure, there is great momentum and promise in seeking to help move the community to a place of greater culturally based resilience, more culturally proficient institutional and grassroots leadership and increased interconnectedness across the various segments of the larger community.

The racial healing and equity initiative rooted in NCN's La Cultura Cura work in Salinas is receiving national attention. Jerry Tello sees this as a promising development in light of recent national events bearing on police-community relations and allied issues of racial injustice. In this context a growing interest has been expressed of late to more forthrightly address the volatile and difficult circumstances the nation has witnessed over recent months in such places as Baltimore,

Maryland; Ferguson, Missouri; Falcon Heights, Minnesota; and Baton Rouge, Louisiana, where police shootings with racial overtones have led to extremely volatile tensions, violence and civil unrest. Cities and regions across California and the nation desperately need new models of effective youth development and community violence prevention. Tello's work through NCN and its partnership with Race Forward offer up a timely alternative to the status quo and a model that is worthy of broader scaling and replication.

Healing Generations

Jerry reminds me that NCN has also partnered effectively with such organizations as Communities for Restorative Youth Justice (CURYJ), the Brotherhood of Elders and allied Native American groups to focus on healing and transforming disparities faced by men and boys of color across races, cultures and generations. NCN and its partners engage elders in the sharing of wisdom and teachings with their younger community counterparts through the Healing Generations program. Participating elders help to lead Círculo healing exchanges involving young men in the community in efforts to become noble men and fathers. The hope and expectation of this work, according to Tello, is to ensure that a growing number of elders, adults and fathers are positioned to mentor and support younger men from the community in ways that reconnect these young males with their authentic, sacred roles vis-à-vis their offspring, their families, their communities and the broader society.

Gathering of Wisdom Keepers

During the balance of our interview, Jerry enthusiastically recounts a recent national gathering of wisdom keepers in Oakland that brought together prominent intergenerational healers, leaders and practitioners from around the country. It was a day of ceremony and teaching. Women elders led off and spoke to the men about what was needed and expected from them in order to heal and strengthen families and communities, so that the next generation could do better. Dialogue and intensive planning using a cross-cultural paradigm focused on distilling a clear direction and priorities for reaching youth.

The convening outcomes and imperatives for healing and improving the life chances for men and boys of color tracked with everything that NCN has been learning about Latino men and boys and assimilating into its various curricula and engagements all across the nation over the years. As Tello recalls, participating adults agreed that the La Cultura Cura model represents much of the medicine young Latino people need today. Youth participants concurred but made clear that what they wished to see is more adult and elder wisdom keepers being more active and accessible to them in their home communities and healing pursuits. As a result, Jerry remembers, the youth themselves called for the formation of a Circle of Wisdom where they could go whenever needed to find supportive adults, elders and healers and where learning, counsel and ceremony would always be available to them.

Establishing a Men and Boys of Color Institute

A few years ago, Jerry Tello pondered with me the idea of establishing an applied research and training institute to do cross-culturally what NCN has been working to do for years on behalf of Latino and indigenous men and boys, as well as their families and communities. It is this reporter's informed opinion that the NCN La Cultura Cura model provides a strong organizational foundation and the core elements of theory and practice required to establish such an institute. Taking encouragement from the recent gathering of wisdom keepers

in Oakland, and building on the many lessons learned from
NCN's work over the past thirty years as a pioneer and leader
in the field of men and boys of color, Tello and his colleagues
have recently decided to formally establish a men and boys of
color institute.

Tello, too, firmly believes that the culturally based resiliency model embedded in the La Cultura Cura framework offers
the necessary philosophical base, values, organizing principles
and innovative practices to effectively advance this work on a
broader scale extending beyond NCN's traditional California-
based work. "The primary mission of the proposed institute,"
explains Tello, "is to promote racial healing and racial equity;
lead efforts to establish work in this area as a legitimate interdisciplinary field of interest; collect, develop and disseminate a
credible body of knowledge; establish criteria for an acknowledged cross-cultural curriculum and training regimen; establish
standards and competencies for professional certification to
advance expert work in the field; provide training and capacity building; and support the creation of more leaders, practitioners and healers trained in La Cultura Cura."

There can be no doubt that one of the great current dilem-
mas facing practitioners in this space is the continuing absence
of more significant scaled investment from government agencies, foundations and private donors. Absent such investment,
leading organizations and networks like NCN will surely continue to succeed and thrive, but not in the more economical
and responsive ways that would be made possible by increased
resource investment and closely aligned field-building efforts.
Meeting the challenge of bringing the work of NCN and others to scale requires support for expanded field capacities in
research, field coordination and training and policy formation—the very things a dedicated institute informed by intercultural, multidisciplinary and intergenerational tenets would

be uniquely situated to advance in this domain. Such an entity could produce expanded field leadership, learning and
demonstrations in policy and best practice, as well as build the
evidence base for efforts to promote the welfare of Latino and
other men and boys of color across the nation.

In effect, the entity that Jerry Tello now intends to develop would position the National Compadres Network to:

- serve as a unifying entity, cultivating and advancing cultural proficiency across the field of Latino and other
  restorative youth justice organizations
- promote culturally based resilience and fluency within
  and between communities
- build a critical mass of intergenerational leaders and
  multidisciplinary, multicultural practitioners versed in
  the La Cultura Cura philosophy and framework
- develop, teach and establish standards of certification
  and use in intercultural and culturally specific curricula
  rooted in the La Cultura Cura framework

The Tello and NCN vision for a new national capacity-
building institute to support youth and community development practitioners interested in Latino and other men and
boys of color stresses the importance of certification in intercultural proficiencies that are rooted in and/or informed by
the La Cultura Cura framework. Tello wants to help establish
recognized national standards and competencies for work in
the field.

Another major focus of the envisioned institute would be
providing ongoing training, convening and initiative support
to Wisdom Keeper Circles (involving elders), Wisdom
Teacher Circles (involving present-generation practitioners
and grassroots activists) and Wisdom Leader Circles (focused

on youth and young adults). Tello's grand design is to support the creation of a critical mass of cross-culturally proficient, intergenerational, multidisciplinary leaders, rooted in their own cultural expression of *In Lak'ech Hala Ken* (innate human interconnectedness), working across the nation to advance real and positive change involving the communities, systems and institutions that are most pivotal in shaping the life course of and opportunities for Latino men and boys.

Reflections and Observations

It is an honor to engage in purposeful conversation with an activist educator, leader and social architect like Jerry Tello. His life's work is manifestly rooted in authentic love, spirituality, purpose, universal truth and principled advocacy in pursuit of our highest humanity. As a writer informed by more than thirty-five years of direct engagement in civil rights, racial equity and community peace, I have had the honor of witnessing amazing efforts to address the many disparities still faced today by families, children and youth of color. It is remarkable to me as I write that such disparities not only persist, but grow and proliferate in our times.

These are not new problems in America. They have been with us for many decades, despite many regular warnings that in the absence of meaningful intervention we are becoming a more divided nation. As a former at-risk youth myself, I know from firsthand experience what is at stake. In my own childhood and youth, I experienced life on the streets. I saw and experienced significant gangland activity, police brutality and real shortcomings in the quality of my early education, health services and job opportunities. I was lucky. I was one of the few from my neighborhood who made it out, completed a good college education and found a way into a solid professional career.

Sadly, too many of the unjust circumstances and disparities I faced myself as a poor child in East Los Angeles and later as a wounded young man of the barrio in the 1960s and early 1970s have remained unchanged. I was blessed to have a warrior mother who instilled in me early and often the medicine of spirituality and *cultura*, although I did not appreciate her many gifts and lessons until much later in life. It took a community activist (Ester Pérez of our local Community Center) and a couple of inspirational neighborhood youth leaders to stir in me the dormant seeds of Chicano identity, indigenous cultural identity and La Cultura Cura.

Then, in 1995, when I joined the California Wellness Foundation as senior staff to that organization's ground-breaking, decade-long Violence Prevention Initiative, I became formally immersed in work to support the true keepers of La Cultura Cura. These keepers of La Cultura Cura and other community peace warriors, including Jerry Tello, José Montoya, Ricardo Carrillo, Samuel Martínez, Isaac Cárdenas, Sammy Núñez, Bobby Verdugo, Armando Lawrence, Mario Ozuna-Sánchez, Héctor Sánchez-Flores, Arnold Perkins, Daniel "Nane" Alejandrez, Walter Guzmán, Luis Rodríguez, Gus Frías, Henry Domínguez, Albino Garcia, Otilio Quintero, Gaylord Thomas, Baba Dodley, Father Greg Boyle, Javier Stauring, Jitu Sadiki, Greg Hodge, George Galvis, Alex Sánchez, Tomas Alejo, Luis Cardona, Ray Gatchalian, Shedrick Sanders and Juan Gómez, are among the forebearers of what is now being called men and boys of color work.

The California Wellness Foundation's ten-year, $100 million investment in promoting a public health framework to address epidemic youth violence changed the national narrative and helped to legitimize a new multidisciplinary field of social investment practice and research. It also provided the comprehensive umbrella of public health science and leadership to help establish the case for more cross-cultural, cross-sector, intergenerational and interdisciplinary work and investment in this arena. Some twenty-five years later, growing legions of multicultural lay and professional public health advocates are doing essential work in addressing the troubling disparities still facing men and boys of color and the communities in which they live. In this connection, the public-health-informed violence prevention movement was vitally important to cultivating a statewide and national cadre of intergenerational, multicultural and interdisciplinary proponents of La Cultura Cura.

Among the aforementioned exemplary youth advocates and community leaders, Jerry Tello has effectively fulfilled the role of elder and headmaster at the people's school of La Cultura Cura. In fact, most of the organizations identified here as leading best practice exemplars have turned to Tello to train their staffs and/or have built their organizational theories of change and core strategies based on the La Cultura Cura framework that Jerry has cultivated and advanced. Largely because of Tello's and NCN's pioneering efforts in the field, allied groups, such as Santa Cruz Barrios Unidos, La Plazita Institute, Homies Unidos, Homeboy Industries and Communities United for Restorative Youth Justice, are now leading regional and national voices on multicultural youth development, violence prevention, gang intervention, restorative justice and community-driven enterprise issues affecting or involving Latino and indigenous men and boys.

The rich body of work presented in this chapter demonstrates NCN's leadership in the field. NCN is presently working in partnership with several leading private foundations on seminal initiatives, including the California Endowment in the context of its Building Healthy Communities place-based initiative and the W. K. Kellogg Foundation in connection with its work in racial equity and healing. In the process, NCN's work is helping to advance a cross-cultural, healing-informed paradigm that will better inform future philanthropic and public investments focused on young men of color. These initiatives can only help to transform for the better the major systems that now too often hinder young Latino men and boys from advancing in American culture and economy, in fields ranging from health and education to child welfare and criminal justice.

NCN's impulse to encourage state and national leaders to create more culturally proficient, strategic and sustainable systems and policy for all men and boys of color—and especially Latino male youth—is both timely and badly needed. The network's recognition as a national leader is well deserved on an unusually broad range of issues, including fatherhood, rites of passage, health, education, family violence, teen pregnancy prevention, cultural competence, juvenile justice, social services, public advocacy, trauma management, healing and evidence-based research. Efficacy and replication in these various realms are essential to any and all comprehensive efforts designed to ameliorate societal disparities and advance the quality of life for Latino, indigenous, black, Asian-Pacific Islander and other men and boys of color.

—

CHAPTER 4

The National Compadres Network and the National Latino Fatherhood & Family Institute

Frank de Jesús Acosta

The National Compadres Network is a nationwide effort whose focus is the reinforcement of the positive involvement of Chicano/Latino/Native males in the lives of their families and communities. As a nonprofit 501(c)(3) organization, the NCN has the mission to strengthen, rebalance and redevelop the traditional compadre extended kinship network by encouraging, supporting and rerooting the positive involvement of males in their families and communities and preventing/reducing the incidence of family and community violence, teen pregnancy, substance abuse and other oppressive behaviors.

As a result of overwhelming need locally and nationally, NCN launched the National Latino Fatherhood & Family Institute (NLFFI). NLFFI serves as the training, technical assistance, policy, advocacy, research and evaluation arm to assist local and national organizations in developing and implementing programs that are culturally competent and draw from the resiliency of Chicano/Latino families and communities. While NLFFI's primary focus is directed at the Chicano/Latino population, the organization has a long history of collaborating with organizations and communities of diverse ethnic backgrounds and is committed to providing services to all boys and men, families and communities. Additional information about the organization, services and resources can be found on their websites at nationalcompadresnetwork.org/ and nlffi.org.

Training and Technical Assistance Services

NLFFI brings together nationally recognized leaders culturally competent in the fields of fatherhood, rites of passage, health, education, family violence, teen pregnancy prevention, cultural competence, juvenile justice, social services, advocacy, trauma, healing and evidence-based research. NLFFI works in partnership with community leaders and decision makers to create strategic and sustainable systems of change and provides support in the areas of training, technical assistance, collective impact building, research, leadership development, resource and material development.

I. Community Healing and Leadership Development Initiatives

A. The Healing Generations Project

The Healing Generations Project expands NLFFI's work to communities that have expressed interest in the Institute's racial and community healing strategies to address persistent community strife and concerns through culturally responsive interventions. It also amplifies the intervention to promote familial community healing through retreats, gatherings and the incorporation of indigenous culturally based practices. NLFFI works with communities to expand this effort through the development of a multitier approach that includes:

- elders of color statewide and local network councils
- trauma informed, healing informed practices

- La Cultura Cura cultural based youth development and rites-of-passage interventions
- Círculo extended kinship support and healing groups

As a result of the intergenerational healing, these communities will begin to coalesce a common voice that advocates for better health/educational outcomes for children, a unified stance against abuse of children and young people, a strong voice against all forms of violence (familial and community) and a leveraging of new resources to support these goals from governmental and nongovernmental organizations.

The Healing Generations Project under the auspices of the National Compadres Network and the Brotherhood of Elders, includes wisdom keepers and community teachers who focus on racial and community healing strategies to address persistent community strife and concerns. Using culturally based healing-informed strategies, they promote familial and community healing via culturally based capacity building, systems change, policy advocacy, retreats and gatherings. Healing Generations works with communities to expand this effort through the development of a multitiered approach that includes the following:

1. Elders council: Strengthens national, statewide and community networks of elders representing diverse communities and ethnicities to develop common ground, build a common voice to deal with community issues and model respectful cross-cultural methods for developing change in their communities.
2. Elders cross-ethnic and cultural healing: Develops gatherings of individuals from diverse communities and cultural backgrounds in order to introduce the concepts of self-healing, sacred manhood and honorable fatherhood.

Trains participants to apply these concepts in an integrated manner within the communities they serve.

3. Next generation youth healing: Develops gatherings of young men from diverse communities and cultural backgrounds to introduce the concepts of self-healing, sacred manhood and honorable fatherhood so that they can identify their positive purpose and desire to serve their families and communities. They learn how to support one another and personally integrate these concepts into their lives.

4. Culturally specific círculos: This phase of the project works with communities to heal internalized oppression and trauma through culturally based healing and learning circles. The effort establishes and expands kinship networks that expose young and adult men to their positive purpose and the positive attributes of manhood and community responsibility. The project networks with existing Círculos to promote the adoption of Círculos in new communities that are self-sustaining and rooted, so that communities take ownership.

B. California Fatherhood Initiative

The goal of the California Fatherhood Initiative (CFI) is to bring together organizations, government entities, professionals, law enforcement, legislators and community advocates who have a vested interest in improving the lives of children, families and communities through positive fatherhood involvement and youth mentorship. CFI's efforts create a unified voice across California to ensure state agencies and departments include services for fathers and young men as a part of their efforts and that organizations throughout the state develop services that are built to serve fathers on the basis of their cultural strengths.

C. Respetar y Leer (Respect and Read) Campaign

Through reading, storytelling and positive involvement by fathers, grandfathers, uncles, older brothers, compadres and other significant males in the lives of children in the community, men standing up against family violence and sitting down to read to their children:

- Reduce the incidence of domestic violence in Chicano/Latino homes. There is a need for men to collectively stand up against family violence.
- Increase the positive involvement of Chicano/Latino males with the children of our community.
- Increase the high school graduation rate of Chicano/Latino children.

D. Men and Women of Honor

Men and Women of Honor is an awareness and healing campaign for war veterans and their families. In conjunction with the American GI Forum of California, Men and Women of Honor work to improve the ability of war veterans to develop and maintain healthy and fulfilling partner and family relationships. Strategies include:

- providing to veterans and their partners presentations on issues and resources related to preventing family violence while developing and maintaining healthy and fulfilling partner and family relationships
- increasing the awareness of veterans and their partners as to how the residual effects of unresolved war trauma can negatively affect their relationships

- helping participants become aware of skills that can assist them in healing trauma related to behaviors that could negatively affect their relationships
- increasing veterans' awareness of available community and online resources that can support their efforts to heal unresolved trauma and prevent family violence

II. Community and Organizational Capacity Building

NLFFI networks with organizations, staff and program leaders and offers culturally competent training and technical assistance in the areas of:

- culturally focused organizational capacity building
- culturally competent community engagement
- program development and inclusion of trauma-informed culturally based practices
- culturally based research and evaluation

III. Policies and Services to Promote Systems Change

The goals are to increase policy-related knowledge of organizations at the local, state and national levels that serve boys, fathers, families and communities and to influence the direction of the fatherhood/male involvement efforts in order to:

- identify existing policy gaps that prevent the development of effective culturally competent fatherhood and male involvement programs
- develop positive culturally competent fatherhood and male involvement policies and programs that build on the cultural strengths of fathers and other male mentors

IV. Culturally Based Curricula

NLFFI has a strong history of successful grant management and program implementation, which has resulted in model programs that have received formal recognition in many communities across the nation. NCN has developed effective and industry-recognized training, technical assistance and curriculum models that are currently in place nationwide.

A. El Joven Noble: The Noble Young Man Rites of Passage Character Development Program

El Joven Noble is a comprehensive, indigenous-based youth leadership development program that supports and guides young men through their manhood rites of passage while focusing on the prevention of substance abuse, teen pregnancy, relationship violence, gang violence and school failure. The program provides a process and a vehicle for the continued rites-of-passage development of youth ages ten to twenty-four. It recognizes that youth need other men/women, their families and communities to care for, assist, heal, guide and successfully prepare them for true manhood/womanhood.

The program incorporates an approach and curriculum that are based on the philosophy of La Cultura Cura. Consistent with this is the belief that rooted in every culture there are protective teachings, traditions and expectations that can assist young men/women across their rites-of-passage bridge. At its base, the Joven program incorporates the indigenous, culturally rooted concept of El Joven Noble, or the Noble Young Man/Woman, and the value of developing and maintaining one's sense of Palabra (Credible Word). In addition, it is believed that in order for youth to be able to develop in this way, they must have positive living examples in their lives as guides, teachers, counselors, elders and supporters. With this in mind, it is the eventual goal of the program to employ and/or incorporate young men and women from the community who have gone through the teachings and have been mentored and trained to deliver direct presentations. More importantly, it is essential that adult men (compadres) and adult women (comadres) serve as guides, teachers and examples in the program to reflect appropriate manhood/womanhood development.

The overall program incorporates a four-phase developmental process, specialized segments (Fire and Water: Violence and Substance Abuse) to address specific areas of need and a parent/family component (Cara y Corazón: Face and Heart) that assists parents in reinforcing the teachings as they heal and grow alongside their youth.

Each participant is guided progressively through the phases and provided with additional teachings as he or she gains in responsibility. The four-phase process includes:

- Phase I: Turtle Circle. Life skills development (Jóvenes con Palabra ten-session format)
- Phase II: Coyote Circle. Cultural identity development
- Phase III: Jaguar Circle. Circle of health and life character development
- Phase IV: Hawk Circle. Leadership/community service development

Finally, an integral component of the program is the development of Círculos de Palabra (Circles of Support), which serve to provide a support and reinforcement process for ongoing healing, growth and development for the young men/women. Ultimately, the entire program attempts to recreate a positive *familia*/community, or extended kinship network, that will allow our youth to develop to their fullest potential.

Curriculum Theoretical Framework. El Joven Noble is a rites-of-passage process based on the indigenous, culturally rooted concept of El Hombre/Mujer Noble and the value of developing and maintaining one's sense of Palabra.

Curriculum Research. The following are the protective factors that this program is intended to enhance:

- Community domain: community rewards for prosocial involvement
- Family domain: family opportunities and rewards for prosocial involvement
- School domain: school opportunities and rewards for prosocial involvement
- Peer and individual domain: character development, social skills and belief in the moral order

Theoretical Formulation. El Joven Noble is divided into four core teachings of development: Conocimiento (Acknowledgement), Entendimiento (Understanding), Integración (Integration) and Movimiento (Movement). These four core teachings directly target parallel risk areas that contribute to the self-destructive behavior of Chicano/Latino youth and other at-risk youth. It is designed to include the physical, emotional, mental and spiritual aspects of each as a basis for direction. Each stage uses a mixture of activities and teaching experiences relating to a young person's self, family and community.

1. Conocimiento: acknowledgment and positive cultural identity development. Chicano/Latino youths live in a world where they have to balance two cultures, and many times they come from families who have experi-

enced generations of racism, discrimination and oppression (social/cultural detachment). Through these oppressive processes, many youth have internalized a negative (false) concept of who they are culturally, and essentially they have learned to "detach" (attachment disorder) from their connection to themselves, their families, their relationships and their own behaviors.

El Joven Noble focuses on a relationship-based process of acknowledging them from an indigenous, cultural perspective, while reinforcing the true essence of who they are and reconnecting them to their authentic potential as Jóvenes Nobles.

2. Entendimiento: understanding of their sacred purpose. In the indigenous beliefs of all traditional cultures, every child is a blessing and has a sacred purpose. However, through living in an oppressive society, many Chicano/Latino youth have come to believe they are high risk, delinquency prone and a burden to their families and society. After generations of thinking this way, many youths have developed internalized oppressive thought patterns and behaviors, causing them difficulty in keeping focused, which they mask by pushing others away (attention deficit, aggressive/reactive behavior). A basic premise of healing, growth and development is the ability of the individual to have a vision of his/her true sacred purpose. If a person only has a negative view of him- or herself, his/her history and his/her culture, then he/she has no avenue for growth and development. He/she must understand the history that has led to the creation of his/her present situation. In this process (narrative reprocessing), and with the proper guidance, he/she will be able to separate pain and dysfunction from

the true essence and teachings that can lead him/her to manifest his/her sacred purpose.

3. Integración: integrating bilingual/bicultural values. Due to the multitude of economic, social and family stressors they experience, many youth live their lives based strictly on survival: getting by, getting over and not getting caught. The clash between the values of the family and those of society often leave youth in the middle, feeling stuck, not learning, not growing (depression) and not motivated to do anything else. On the other hand, positive values, a love for life and a circle of support (Círculo de Hombres/Mujeres) are the basis for learning, healing, growing and leading others. As times change, people must learn new ways (based on ancient teachings) to be able to analyze and process the changing world's demands without losing a sense of their culture and ethnic connection. Living with a sense of spirit (spirituality) and *ganas* (internal strength) allows one to deal with difficult and overwhelming pressures with a sense of hope and vision.

4. Movimiento: safety, security and interconnected trust. Fear is one of the greatest obstacles many youth face today. Living in dangerous neighborhoods, where gangs, drug use and violence are prevalent, creates ongoing insecurity and anxiety (anxiety disorders, posttraumatic stress), which many times spill into their relationships as well. Young people need continual adult mentorship and a place to go (Círculos) to release burdensome issues in an environment where supportive adults can teach them positive life skills and assist them in navigating their rites of passage into manhood/womanhood.

Finally, these youth must understand the significant role they play in protecting, guiding and leading the next generation, so that they may one day become future Joven Noble facilitators.

B. Cara y Corazón: Face and Heart Family Strengthening Program

Cara y Corazón is a culturally based family strengthening/community mobilization program that assists parents and other extended family to raise and teach their children with a positive bicultural base.

C. Padres con Cara y Corazón: Fathers with Face and Heart

The Padres con Cara y Corazón program focuses on guiding and supporting fathers to develop an active, positive, nurturing relationship with their children while assisting them to deal with the day-to-day struggles of fatherhood.

D. Raising Children with P.R.I.D.E.: A Teen Fatherhood Program

Raising Children with P.R.I.D.E. is a comprehensive, multicultural young-fatherhood program (coauthored by Dr. Marilyn Steele) that assists new or expectant fathers in becoming positive influences in the lives of children and family while assisting them in dealing with the multitude of challenges they face.

E. Hombres Nobles Buscando Balance: Nobel Men Looking for Balance

Hombres Nobles Buscando Balance is a domestic violence intervention process with the goal of guiding men toward family harmony and healing from family violence. This comprehensive, culturally based intervention program (coauthored by Dr. Ricardo Carrillo, Samuel Martínez and Rolando Reyna Goubeau) is focused on working with men who have relationship violence as an issue in their lives.

F. Mama's Love: Mothers Raising Honorable Boys

Mama's Love is a curriculum-focused program assisting mothers to develop a positive relationship with their sons and guide them to be honorable young men.

G. Fire and Water

The Fire and Water curriculum is a segment of the overall Joven Noble rites-of-passage program that works with young people who have major issues of anger/violence (fire) and substance abuse (water).

V. Culturally Competent Resource Materials

The organization has developed bilingual/bicultural brochures on the following topics:
- male health
- sexual health
- teen pregnancy prevention
- preventing male cancers
- detecting diabetes
- avoiding alcoholism
- substance abuse
- preventing HIV/AIDS
- fatherhood lessons

The NLFFI's Latino fatherhood tools include a fatherhood toolkit designed by service practitioners with a personal understanding of Latino culture to offer proven strategies and interventions to help Latino men of all ages strengthen and heal their families. In addition, NLFFI has made available fatherhood posters on the themes of "A Noble Man," "A True Macho" and "Your Greatest Work" (Native American fatherhood).

CHAPTER 5

Albino García, Jr., La Plazita Institute

Interview by Frank de Jesús Acosta

I first met Albino García, Jr. while he was working as a senior staff person at Santa Cruz Barrios Unidos in the mid-1990s. He was the person who took the organization's values and principles (which were philosophically rooted in the cultural sovereignty of the Chicano movement) and built a change strategy and core curriculum for Barrios Unidos based on La Cultura Cura. He drew heavily on Jerry Tello's framework (highlighted earlier in this volume), particularly the National Compadres Network's Joven Noble model featuring the traditions of talking circles and ceremony. I vividly remember Albino telling me about this work and its associated challenges back when he was still freshly going through much of the healing and transformation of living a sober and principled life himself—literally learning to live the philosophy.

It is a true test for the gang organizer (and an absolute requirement of the work) to look wounded and lost young brothers and sisters in the eye from a place of integrity. It is difficult but essential work in turn to challenge these young people to change their ways, to dig down and find life principles that are buried so deep inside their damaged hearts and souls they cannot even comprehend their presence within. Chicago native Albino García, Jr. understands this challenge and charge personally and profoundly, based on his long-standing leadership on the front lines of Chicano gang prevention and intervention work in and around his ancestral home city of Albuquerque, New Mexico. In a conversation in 2006 to inform the writing of my 2007 book on the history of the Barrios Unidos movement, Albino shared the following thoughts and perspectives:

> The codes of the gang and streets are crystal clear. I believed we needed to set our own clear standards by getting the young people's *palabra* (word or oath) that they were going to do what it took to change destructive behaviors and to learn a new way. We wanted their *palabra* of loyalty to the values of *cultura* (culture), a commitment to try new things and work hard, to have respect for school traditions and sacred rituals, showing *ganas* (desire), personal responsibility and an obligation that transcended colors.
>
> The youth had to understand that they had to give up something (allegiance to a counterfeit culture and destructive behaviors) to get something in return (the beautiful birthrights of their heritage and an opportunity for new life). The only evidence we had to back up our promise of a better life was our own personal example. It was one thing to design a curriculum; it was another to train everyone and get them on the same page. I felt staff had to know the curriculum cold and certainly had to model what they were trying to teach. We had some folks working or volunteering at Barrios (Santa Cruz Barrios Unidos, or BU) who were still walking in both worlds (the world of the streets from which they came and the world we were trying to create at BU). We wanted our staff and volunteers to not

only teach our methods of change, but also to model our values and principles in their own behavior—in essence, to walk the talk.

Teaching the philosophy and principles of La Cultura Cura from a place of deep understanding and credibility demands the instructor be a dedicated practitioner: a living, breathing example of someone who has faced his own brokenness and frailties but who has nevertheless evolved. By offering medicine that they find within themselves, buried deep inside a damaged heart and soul, the dedicated practitioner can help to create a pathway enabling still-troubled souls around them to realize their own humanity and a better way of life. Albino put it well when he told me in one of our conversations some years ago, "In healing, we discover the sacred light within ourselves, becoming able to see the sacred light in others."

As I reflect on my conversations with Albino for this book, I recall our first meeting. He greeted me with the barrio handshake, at once showing a curiosity and an inquiring glare that could only come from one homeboy sizing up another. I do not think Albino cared one bit about my then professional standing as a leading representative of the California Wellness Foundation, Barrios Unidos' major funder at the time. Instead, he was looking into my heart and my soul; he was trying to take stock of me as a man and one of the still relatively few Chicanos back then (it was the late 1990s) in a position to provide culturally competent, meaningful and useful resources to our communities.

I would like to think he eventually determined that I came from a place of *cultura* and *espíritu*. It bodes well that he still trusts me (as a scribe of our community's history and contemporary reality in America) to tell authentic stories for our people and to share the work of La Plazita on the public record. Albino is by heart a storyteller in his own right and a holy man (a sun dancer and ceremonial chief of Apache and Chichimec heritage). For the purposes of this publication, I asked him the same three research questions I posed to Jerry Tello, whose leading work with the National Compadres Network is also featured in this volume. When I previewed the foundational questions that were intended to drive our interview, he laughed disarmingly and said they were a bit heady and complex. Nevertheless, he agreed to just start talking, sharing stories and reflecting upon his work with the hope that his replies would meet my investigation's purposes. The following is what resulted from our exchange.

Why must American society better understand and respond to the social and economic disparities faced by Latino men and boys?

Albino began his response to my initial question by posing a rhetorical question of his own to American society at large. "If we, as a collective people, truly believe in the basic tenets of equity, justice, freedom and pluralism," he queried, "then how can we stand by idly when nearly one-quarter of our people are living in such disparity?" His profundity and precision in response were not unexpected, but they were provocative and unusually powerful. This is the essence of what it takes to be an authentic leader of a people or a movement—clarity of purpose and voice. Albino García, Jr. is such a leader.

It is important for every individual of integrity to acknowledge the objective truth. Despite the values our nation professes to the world, the daily reality of life for most Chicanos, Latinos, Native people, African Americans and other people of color living in the United States has very seldom reflected the full benefit of these ideals. Albino believes it is important for mainstream white America to understand what this does to us as people of color. Latinos of Native descent fundamentally value equity and justice as part of our ancestral cultural heritage. The daily expression of these cultural values is important to our well-being, just as they are to people from any other culture. What those involved in the La Cultura Cura movement are doing is healing the human and communal damage that generations of oppression and disparity have done while reawakening, teaching and living more progressive human and social virtues. This is important not only for the survival and benefit of our people but also for the well-being of *all* people.

As we discuss the reasons why America must act to better address the needs of Latino and other men and boys of color, Albino shares a story. It concerns a Chicano and Native eighteen-year-old young man who only recently came to La Plazita Institute (LPI), located in Albuquerque, New Mexico, to seek redemption and support. Albino warns me: "This isn't a pretty story with a happy ending." Nevertheless, he goes on to say, "what the story reflected, is the brokenness, anger, desperation and nihilism we encounter too much in our barrios and reservations here in New Mexico and throughout the US."

As the story went, the young man came to LPI as the result of the organization's community-wide restorative justice work in and around Albuquerque. Owing in large part to LPI's effective advocacy in the community and the work of allied groups, where nonserious offenses are involved, young at-risk Latinos like the one in question are now increasingly being referred directly to leading community-based support centers, like LPI, instead of being incarcerated in juvenile corrections facilities (as was the local practice for many decades).

The youth in question was a beneficiary of this important reform in process and punishment. Because his infractions were relatively few and minor, he was accordingly assigned by the juvenile court to participate in LPI's healing and developmental probation program. Like any other young person or adult who comes to the institute for service or restoration, the young man received care, instruction, counseling and service-learning opportunities in a supportive environment. But despite showing general improvement, the young LPI newcomer kept falling into troubling behavior, expressing deeply rooted anger and continuing to be involved with the negative influences in his neighborhood.

An elder at LPI, who knew the youth's family and had an ear to the community beat, pulled the young man aside. Out of concern, the elder asked the youth how he was doing, mentioning certain rumors others had been broadcasting about the young man getting back into the things that had initially produced his troubles with the law. The youth's answer was volatile and immediate. He responded with unreasonable anger and even the threat of retaliatory violence. After receiving counsel from several LPI staff and volunteer healers, the youngster eventually ended up in Albino's office. The meeting was difficult, but it went well enough, and, with great hope, the young man was returned to the program.

But the story did not end there. Although the troubled youth seemed to move forward with his life, something else was going on behind the scenes. Coming from a very poor home, the young man had surreptitiously taken to illegally selling marijuana in order to make ends meet and help financially at home. His parents and family were unaware; and the extent of the problem was masked during the ensuing months, even as the young man delved ever more deeply into illegal activity that clearly violated his court-ordered probation. Unfortunately, the worst finally caught up with the young offender, and the moment that every community worker and advocate dreads came to be.

Late one night Albino received a call from the young man's mother, crying and saying that the police were looking for her son as a suspect in a violent attack on another individual. It turned out the young man had been cornered by a local gang leader and, in fear for his life, had put a hatchet in the neck of his attacker. Presently, the young man who perpetrated the crime is in custody. Fortunately, the person whom he injured survived the attack, although not without severe lasting wounds. LPI continues to provide support to the mother as well as counseling the offending youth, who turned himself in to authorities. Advocates are standing by the youngster, fighting for his freedom under a plea of self-defense. He faces a long stretch of prison time if he is found guilty. The case is still pending.

Perhaps in order to avoid facing our own pain and discomfort about cases like this one, many in America, including even those close to our communities and their issues, romanticize the prospects of redeeming and restoring young men like the one just featured in Albino's story. But real life is not so tidy and kind. Working with at-risk young people produces constant back-and-forth successes and challenges. The pathway to peace is rarely an even and immediate one for these youth and teens. There are no excuses for their propensity to struggle and fail along their pursuit of the path; but there are valid explanations, given the cultures of poverty, crime and violence these young Americans have inherited through no real fault of their own. Working with these young people accordingly requires unusually healthy doses of love and patience, tolerance and grace.

As Albino García sees it, "Regardless of how far our young people fall, we must keep working to heal and guide them, to offer the medicine that will lead them to their authentic cul-

ture and sacred self. We need to bring them back into the circle of family and community." The assumption underlying
much mainstream institutional response to Latino and Native
youth is that they are so far detached from what is good and
right, they are not worthy people. But for those of us who
know and love these young ones, who know their innate
sacredness and potential, this is an unacceptable injustice and
a failure of the entire society. When proper nurturing, rooted
in love, touches these young people where their traditional
identity and culture reside, a beautiful and remarkable blos-
soming of humanity occurs.

Albino points out that many of the recognized elders and
emerging leaders of the La Cultura Cura and related movements (e.g., those focused on supporting and advancing community peace, restorative justice, immigrants' rights and men
and boys of color) had to be transformed themselves, laying to
rest their own issues and demons. In fact, many of the foremost
leaders in this space, like Albino, are themselves recovered (or
recovering) addicts, former gang members, ex-offenders and/or
at-risk, disaffected youth. They are living examples of the
power of La Cultura Cura, working to create the path to support a growing intergenerational, cross-cultural army of leaders, multidisciplinary practitioners, teachers, healers, counselors and grassroots activists—all in service to the cause of
community building and peace.

**The best practice models profiled in the book series are
all self-identified as culturally based and rooted in La
Cultura Cura. What is the evidence that these so-called
best practice strategies actually work?**

As our conversation continues, Albino reminds me that
he is only one of many elders and pioneers whose work has
helped to shape the La Cultura Cura movement. He readily

acknowledges both his mentors and his contemporaries in the field, such as Jerry Tello, "Nane" Alejandrez, Luis Rodríguez, Magdaleno Rose-Avila and Henry Domínguez, among others. All of these leaders, guided by the values and principles of La Cultura Cura, have made fundamental contributions to furthering the knowledge base beyond what Latino activists have traditionally been taught through our grassroots organizing, movement building, youth advocacy and community institutional development efforts. The journey for these pioneers has not been easy as they have worked for change in a chauvinistic social environment that still largely considers Latinos to be an inferior subculture.

As Albino recounts it to me, for most of the past thirty years since his and others' work in the field commenced, the *cultura* medicine these leaders employed in schools, correctional systems, health and social service systems, churches and community settings was not fully recognized or given legitimacy. In effect, they advanced the field's substance and legitimacy, not because of any institutional backing or support, but, rather, because of their own perseverance in the face of significant institutional resistance. "When we all started," Albino explains, "we didn't have a construct or model that organized the language, translated the concepts or established a framework of working principles; we were building a body of new knowledge as we worked. He continues:

> Many of the earlier practitioners of La Cultura Cura worked together and with field leaders like Jerry Tello to translate our *cultura* into understandable language, concepts and a comprehensive framework that could be used intraculturally and cross-culturally to transform lives, systems and policies. We wanted to create

equitable, just and life-affirming communities for boys and men of color and all people.

As reported here in the previous chapter, Jerry Tello of the National Compadres Network has spent the last forty years developing, teaching, testing, applying, learning, innovating and concretizing the La Cultura Cura model. Tello's seminal Joven Noble curriculum served as a guide in the field for operationalizing the model's philosophy, values, principles and practices into an accessible and applicable body of knowledge. The subsequent allied work of pioneering groups, such as Barrios Unidos and La Plazita, founded by alumni of the NCN model, have laid the foundation for what is now increasingly accepted best practice and evidence-based work in the men and boys of color field.

Indeed, NCN created among the nation's first model frameworks for transforming at-risk Latino and Native American individuals, families, communities and systems. In recent years, this work has been widely recognized as evidence based and has been shown to produce unusually effective outcomes that are difficult to match via other approaches to youth development and restoration. La Plazita has adapted this philosophy and framework to its local community in New Mexico.

A quick snapshot shows that La Plazita serves Albuquerque's most vulnerable youth and adult populations and their families. Participants are primarily of Latino, Chicano and Native American heritage. Many have been previously incarcerated and/or gang involved, and the vast majority come from families with multigenerational legacies of poverty, gang involvement and addiction. LPI is recognized throughout the state of New Mexico for reducing violence, addiction, incarceration and recidivism among the most overrepresented youth and adults in detention, including those considered high risk.

One of the reasons for the persistence of these problems in Latino communities in and around Albuquerque, Albino tells me, is that too many of the people served by LPI fall through the cracks of conventional social service institutions. Typically, he observes, social service agencies operate in silos that are disconnected from the wholeness of who these young people are as human beings. Too often, they treat the individual in isolation from his culture, community and clan. LPI serves entire families and kinship circles with culturally based support that facilitates both collective healing and the development of the individual's core identify and well-being.

A more underlying reason why the problems LPI treats persist is related to racial segregation and poverty. The primary communities served by LPI are located in South Valley (a locality situated in the southwest quadrant of Bernalillo County), which is overwhelmingly Latino. As we continue our exchange, Albino informs me that South Valley has long been a regional center of Latino community suffering and hardship. Many South Valley residents are of extremely low socioeconomic status, with all the attendant disparity-related risk factors that typically follow that designation.

Above all, local residents experience poor health, inadequate education and irregular, low-paid employment. Over two-thirds of South Valley's children thus live in households with incomes below the federal poverty level. Fully 25 percent of the overall South Valley population presently lives in poverty. Three local water sources had to be closed by federal regulators in the 1980s because of high toxicity levels; yet, still today, the area remains on the US Environmental Protection Agency's list of Superfund sites, needing ongoing remedial actions to contain, capture and reduce concentrations of the contaminant plume within the local ground water.

In this context, alternatives to gangs, drugs and crime are few and far between where local Latino youth are concerned. As a result, positive spaces and places are badly needed in order to provide local youth and their families with needed comfort, opportunities, support and hope. LPI is described as a cultural "hub" for area youth, adults and families who attend weekly ceremonies and programs in education, arts, health, conservation and entrepreneurship (in such product and service areas as organic farming, ceramics, silk-screen design and community health services). The LPI organizational framework flows entirely from the La Cultura Cura construct. The community that LPI serves otherwise lacks authentic culturally based resources aimed at remedying its social and economic challenges.

Because of the nature and extent of the problems facing local youth in LPI's service zone, comprehensive, rather than isolated, interventions are required. I ask Albino to tell me about the breadth of LPI's programs, strategies and activities that respond to this reality. But Albino tells me the institute's restorative justice work with juveniles serves as the essential prism from which one can glean the core values and principles that guide all of LPI's work. So he focuses his comments on that important body of work.

LPI Restorative Justice Approach

Albino García, Jr. does not believe that America's juvenile and criminal justice systems can be the leaders or architects of their own reform toward a restorative justice model. In his view, the principal leaders and stakeholders of that universe are too wedded to conventional detainment and policing practices that are fundamentally at odds with the best interests of Latinos and other men and boys of color across the nation. At the same time, Albino acknowledges in his exchange with me that an authentic partnership must ultimately be forged to constructively engage law enforcement, its leadership and its rank-and-file personnel as members of the communal family. Albino tells me that producing the space for such an alignment with traditionally hostile law enforcement leaders and agencies requires a holistic approach to cross-cultural (re)education, training and planning. Cultivating trust within a community that has been largely "misserved" by local law enforcement and justice practices requires substantial healing, reorientation and trust building across all sectors. The task is not easy, as Albino confides, but it is essential work that LPI has begun to undertake by beginning to introduce select law enforcement personnel to the healing powers of La Cultura Cura, using ritual and inclusive dialogues to advance collective support for restorative justice's values, principles and application in real-life situations.

In this work, LPI has played the essential role of intermediary in what Albino calls an environment of "hateful complexity." It is no simple endeavor to erase the legacy of injustice in sentencing and mass incarceration. Where Latinos and other communities of color are concerned (and especially our at-risk youth), the law enforcement, justice and education systems have been more adversarial than cooperative. The dance of objectivity and neutrality in facilitating the creation of a new form of relationship between community and commanding institutions like the police, the courts and the schools is difficult for any grassroots advocacy organization. LPI nevertheless hosts monthly meetings with law enforcement and court officials, as well as education and civic leaders, in an atmosphere of *cultura*—in a communal and ceremonial fashion.

These unique and powerful exchanges bring together all sectors within the community and local law enforcement to seek mutual understanding and enhanced cooperation based on restorative, rather than punitive, approaches to the greatest extent possible. The sessions include at-risk youth and adults, family and interested community members, juvenile justice court staff, judges, juvenile probation officers, prosecutor and district attorney staff, public defenders, correctional facility leaders, education system leaders and local safety net providers.

This groundbreaking work establishes the space for finding collective voice in support of the restorative justice model. It is not merely a one-way street designed to attend solely to the pain and needs of Latino youth and community members. On the contrary, the sessions invite reciprocity and authenticity that extends to the significant benefit of participating local and county officials and other civic and community leaders, most of whom are not residents of South Valley. Albino tells me this is to address what he calls "trauma on the institutional side." By this he is referring to the layers of draconian laws of recent decades, such as minimum mandatory sentencing requirements and forced youth transfers to adult prison facilities that actually preclude institutional agents of the justice system from contributing to the healing, restoration and corrections policy reforms that are so badly needed in our times.

García tells me that, metaphorically and ironically, the punitive system that has prevailed over the decades until now effectively handcuffs the criminal justice system's own agents and prevents them from exercising their natural human instincts of compassion and reason in the dispensation of their duties to protect and to serve. It systematically compels these actors to make decisions that real life evidence makes clearer and clearer are at odds with the basic tenets of our democracy and common sense. The current restrictive state of affairs in conventional law enforcement and the administration of justice thus prevents groups like LPI from joining forces with sympathetic district attorneys, prosecutors, judges, probation officers and defense attorneys. Presently, even professional law enforcement leaders and practitioners of goodwill, heart and conscience cannot follow restorative values or avenues; instead, they are compelled to follow only the color of law. Fortunately, the swing of the political pendulum has opened a window to reform; and this in turn has allowed LPI and other leading groups to open up new space for experimentation through innovations like the alternative youth sentencing practices the local courts have introduced in recent years and the powerful circles of community and law enforcement leaders coming together in La Cultura Cura exchanges under LPI's auspices. Albino tells me that what makes these changes possible is mutuality. He underscores the need for both sides—community and law enforcement—to examine their own appropriate degrees of culpability, responsibility and accountability for the present situation's prolongation. Ownership for individual and collective accountability are cornerstone tenets of restorative justice.

Nevertheless, none of this means that culpability is necessarily an even proposition in the relationship between local police and law enforcement on the one hand and aggrieved families and community interests on the other. The reality is that virtually all of the conventional power in terms of resourcing, authority and force resides in the police rather than in the people. And this reality is further reinforced by the very depth of local challenges and disadvantages confronting LPI, its service population and its community partners relative to law enforcement and justice issues. The data speak for themselves: Albuquerque holds the dubious distinction of having among the nation's highest ratio of school dropouts to criminal detentions.

The singular unifying goal for the restorative justice movement is, not assigning blame, but rather changing social reality. LPI therefore does not see itself as a social service agency or even as a social justice organization—although it would not be unfair to characterize it as either. Above all, LPI sees itself as an agent for transformational change. In order to move its restorative justice work forward, LPI deploys its full cadre of programs and services aimed at both juvenile justice reform and broader strategies to build change leading to the greater social, political and economic empowerment of Latino and allied indigenous peoples across New Mexico and the Southwestern United States.

To complement its role as a regional intermediary and catalyst, LPI activities include services that

- provide traditional healing and cultural services to incarcerated Latino and Native youth and adults through purification sweat lodge and pipe ceremonies within various correctional institutions (including the Juvenile Detention Center, Bernalillo County Metropolitan Detention Center and Santa Fe Adult Detention Center) as well as on-site at La Plazita Institute
- enhance and expand outreach, support and mentoring groups, educational programming, community engagement and healing circles to high-risk, adjudicated, post-incarcerated local youth and their families
- bolster opportunities for youth, adults, inmates, ex-offenders and families to engage in meaningful individual and collective advancement through education and job training programs, professional and trade associations, policy advocacy networks, entrepreneurship circles and projects in language, arts and crafts
- advance collective impact work with policy makers, judicial system representatives and community members

to reduce race-based disparities among Latino, Chicano and Native American youth and adult inmates

Following below are brief overviews of LPI's core programs and priorities, as well as associated descriptions, which reflect its broad range of institutional modalities.

Rudolfo Anaya Urban Barrio Youth Corps

A tangible sign of endorsement and recognition relative to the LPI's work, based on evidence of its impacts and benefits in the local community, resides in its most recent program innovation— the Rudolfo Anaya Urban Barrio Youth Corps. With financial support totaling $50,000 from the national organization Hispanics in Philanthropy, La Plazita Institute has established its important new program center for youth and young men ages sixteen to twenty-five. The program seeks to engage adjudicated, disconnected or otherwise at-risk young people exhibiting promising and enterprising service to their community. The intent is to help these young people build on their innovations and service inclinations by providing them with tangible, hands-on training and work experience, as well as access to transformative holistic learning experiences, networks and opportunities.

Program participation requires involved youth to complete conservation service projects on ancestral tribal lands and waterways, located on the historic Town of Atrisco Land Grant (Merced). La Plazita fields crews of Latino, Chicano and Mexican participants, comprised in each instance of four members and two leaders. The project supports community-based conservation efforts to protect and restore local habitats and natural areas, enhance water quality and promote traditional and cultural urban farming and agricultural practices. It also provides transformative educational, professional and technical training to Latino youth and community leaders on sustainable and indigenous agricultural practices.

Indeed, the youth corps experience deliberately exposes participating youth to applied research, community engagement and advocacy techniques that help them to support locally based community agricultural projects. The goal is to enhance their stewardship capacities on public and private agricultural lands in order to improve local water quality and to maintain and reinvigorate agricultural productivity across the region. This component of the Barrio Youth Corps program seeks to address local inequities by protecting the health and safety of those involved in food and farm systems. The project also promotes education to establish reductions (or elimination) of toxic materials in agricultural production processes.

AgriCultura Network

La Plazita is cofounder of the Agri-Cultura Network, which contracts with Albuquerque Public Schools to provide quality organic food to students, schools and community members who may not otherwise have access to healthy food products. In 2015, La Plazita negotiated a new contract with the Bernalillo County Youth Services Center to become a local vendor providing detained youth with certified organic produce as part of an effort to make healthy meals available daily to these young people.

In addition, LPI's La Cosecha program (*cosecha* means "harvest") delivers organic parcels each week to 250 community members and families. The project is committed to maintaining certified organic status for the benefit of low-income families and those youth and elders who are further marginalized through incarceration. The goal is to develop infrastructure for a new community-supported agricultural program (CSA) at three new farm sites recently donated by local residents, heirs and community organizations to bolster urban agricultural systems and promote economic and community development within Bernalillo County and the Town of Atrisco. The desired outcomes of this remarkable body of work and innovation are worth enumerating. They include:

• reduction of race-based and ethnic disparities among Latino and Native youth through engagement in critical prevention work and collaborative policy reform efforts involving local, state and national stakeholders
• development and implementation of culturally appropriate strategies and best practices to reform the juvenile and criminal justice systems
• provision of meaningful and sustainable job opportunities that expose young people—and especially urban, tribal and minority youth—to the natural world and related career opportunities in conservation, agriculture and science, technology, engineering and math
• reinvigoration of agricultural systems, as well as economic- and community-development efforts, through programs that focus on poverty alleviation, food sovereignty, social justice and land and water reclamation
• restoration of local urban youths' connections to their agricultural heritage through social enterprise and entrepreneurship
• augmentation of local families' and youths' access to affordable organic produce through a community-supported agricultural program

Multiple Worlds Leadership Program

The Multiple Worlds Leadership Program (MWLP) is offered to anyone who qualifies for participation in LPI programs and services. The MWLP is rooted in the core values of community culture, wisdom and history. The program, specifically designed for youth, adults and elders, is based on the premise that everyone has the inherent power to maneuver in and out of a variety of environments—thus the concept of "multiple worlds."

The experience creates space for youth participants, facilitators and elders to pursue a journey of self-discovery that leads to an enhanced sense of identity, ownership and belonging among individuals who have lost touch with or been denied teachings about their core cultural identity. The program highlights five centers, or "worlds," of focus to establish a context for lifelong learning and growth. In essence, this is a journey to gain understanding of one's self, first by unlearning what is harmful and then by relearning what is innate in the individual's ancestral/cultural world view. The "worlds" encompass the following meanings and purposes:

- First World: Look internally for answers, seek the authentic self.
- Second World: Treat one another as mutually linked and dependent—the practice of *In Lak'ech Hala Ken* (I am the other you, and you are the other me).
- Third World: Extend *In Lak'ech* to others outside of your normal *cultura* and circles of influence.
- Fourth World: Understand systems and institutions for the purpose of moving and strengthening our world.
- Fifth World: Maintain well-being of self, family, community, systems and society.

Within each stage of the MWLP curricula, the themes of spirituality, civic engagement, community, diversity and leadership are addressed and defined through the lens of La Cultura Cura. The curriculum is intended to reconnect youth, adults and elders to one another within the Latino, Chicano and Native American communities through rites of passage, learning rituals, ceremony and symbols. LPI's process takes participants through a journey of self-discovery that helps them to develop empathy for others, while at the same time providing them with the nuanced skills required to maneuver effectively across different worlds.

Participating youth become stronger and more informed representatives of their own culture within these multiple worlds, thus enhancing their sense of self and their potential for community and civic leadership. They are challenged to think critically and to develop their own definitions of leadership, community, service and public responsibility. The main thrust of this work is to expand participating young people's world views beyond the idea that they are mere passive participants in their lives and society. Instead, this work seeks to encourage participating youth to become effective agents of change.

What are key challenges, opportunities and priorities for the Latino boys and men of color in your community and nationwide?

In the final stages of my interview with Albino to inform this publication, he turned to my third and last interview question, not with a story or another description of a comprehensive LPI program strategy, but rather with a passionate desire to focus on the institute's articulated target outcomes for work in restorative justice. These, he told me, are generally reflective of outcomes that would surface in any community working comprehensively to change the disparities faced by men and boys of color. Such outcome goals are indicative of the systems change, policy change, community change and social change that leaders of La Cultura Cura all ultimately seek.

What is distinctive about LPI's work, like the work of Jerry Tello that is highlighted in the previous chapter, is that it is increasingly well documented on the public record in ways that promise to ensure its future study, replication and adaptation across the national field of youth empowerment advocacy. Albino's outcomes list (included below), although simple, identifies the fundamental elements that provide for the equity, justice, humanity, self-sufficiency and dignity of millions of people in our nation who have been systematically denied their inalienable birthrights to these and other public goods. The challenges for us now are to assess the waning state of our democracy in America and to apply our collective assets to advance needed changes in society that better serve both men and boys of color and, in the process, *all* Americans.

LPI Restorative Justice Proposed Outcomes

- Build institutional and organizational collaboration through training and coaching so that all partners are aware of the special concerns of the Latino youth population and systemic barriers as well as the assets and strengths of the community.
- Improve equity in racial, ethnic, health, education and economic disparities among Latino youth in Bernalillo County.
- Become an evidence-based model of successful social entrepreneurship showing how to engage disconnected youth with positive and healthy supportive systems, thereby improving overall health and well-being through economic enterprise.

- Advance positive youth engagement. Participants demonstrate resiliency, attitudinal and/or belief-system changes (e.g., sense of positive belief in future, positive self-esteem, connection to social, educational, workforce and community networks, goal setting).
- Promote GED/diploma completion while serving in the Barrio Youth Corps and/or establish education plan within thirty days after finishing the program.
- Discourage court and criminal involvement (technical violation of supervised release, diversion program, conviction, revocation and reincarceration).
- Maintain a drug-free status or engage in drug treatment and/or substance abuse education and, if positive, successfully participate in community supervision sanctions, alternatives to detention or other diversion programs.
- Complete job readiness training and professional, trade and technical skill development (including soft and transferable skills).
- Increase capacity of Community Supported Agricultural program developments through the provision and acquisition of resources and farm operation materials. Establish strong coordinated and aligned efforts for La Plazita Gardens and establish first cohort of members, shareholders and overall planning and infrastructure.
- Distribute locally grown organic produce, generating new produce sales.
- Create mechanisms by which families can apply SNAP and WIC benefits to purchase produce.
- Recruit twenty households to participate in CSA's pilot season, with the help of partner organizations.

- Recruit community support for the project to ensure second season capacity and to raise community awareness.
- Provide all promotional materials in both English and Spanish.
- Increase awareness and stakeholder support of pilot CSA and strengthen efforts with newsletters, information, resource materials and interactive education activities, including community cooking classes and events at La Plazita Gardens.
- Strengthen capacity within Bernalillo County criminal justice, behavioral health and related social services systems to reduce adjudication and recidivism overall and address economic, education and health disparities.
- Build collaborative linkages among community services relevant to this youthful population, their families and social networks.

CHAPTER 6

La Plazita Institute Organizational Overview

Frank de Jesús Acosta

La Plazita Institute serves the most often marginalized populations in our community, including Hispanic/Latino, Chicano and Mexican immigrant families, urban Native Americans (intertribal) and citizens returning to the community from incarceration. The primary focus of La Plazita Institute is residents that live in the southwest quadrant of Bernalillo County. The extraordinarily low socioeconomic status of many South Valley residents is one of the main risk factors for numerous adverse health and social effects. A full two-thirds of the children in the South Valley live in households with income below the federal poverty line. Among local elementary schools as many as 95 percent of South Valley students receive subsidized lunches. Additionally, the South Valley population comprises the largest number of adjudicated and incarcerated youth and adults in New Mexico.

The population lends itself to changing patterns of fertility, mortality, education, economics, family structure and migration, all of which have a profound impact on the population's health and the social, educational and cultural services that are typically difficult for vulnerable populations to obtain and navigate. LPI offers traditional healing and nontraditional programs in the Bernalillo County Juvenile Detention Center, Bernalillo County Metropolitan Detention Center and Santa Fe Adult Detention Center. For example, there are more than 600 incarcerated Native Americans within these facilities. Despite being the smallest segment of the population, Native Americans have the second largest state prison incarceration rate in the nation, according to a recent review of prison statistics. In terms of language, more than 31 percent of the total Bernalillo County population speaks a language other than English, primarily Spanish, hence the necessity to provide culturally appropriate, accessible and affordable resources to the affected community.

Mission

La Plazita Institute is a nonprofit grassroots organization in Albuquerque. La Plazita engages New Mexico's youth, elders and communities in a comprehensive, holistic and cultural approach. Designed around the philosophy of La Cultura Cura, La Plazita's programs engage New Mexico's youth, elders and communities to draw from their own roots and histories in order to express core traditional values of respect, honor, love and family.

History

Since 2004, LPI has provided cultural healing services to Albuquerque's most vulnerable youth and adult populations and their families. Most participants are of Hispanic/Latino, Chicano and Native American heritage, have been previously incarcerated and/or gang involved and come from families with multigenerational legacies of poverty, gang involvement and substance abuse and addiction.

There is an enormous need for this work, as our population tends to fall through the cracks of conventional social service institutes. Accordingly, LPI provides whole family, culturally appropriate support to facilitate healing and the development of core identity and self-esteem. LPI is a cultural hub for urban Native American families who attend weekly Inipi ceremonies and language and arts and crafts programs.

La Plazita has made huge strides in establishing a significant footprint in the South Valley and throughout the state of New Mexico by reducing violence, addiction, incarceration and recidivism among the most overrepresented youth and adults in detention and those considered high-risk populations within the community.

The seeds, successes and sustainability achieved in strengthening the social, physical and cultural capital of the South Valley can be attributed to the expertise and diligence of La Plazita staff, community leadership, volunteers and students, as well as the funding support provided by many public and private donors and community partners committed to LPI's mission and vision. In addition, collective impact, coalition building and systemic and social change are central to the efforts La Plazita Institute is engaged in.

Organizational Goals

- Improve the health and well-being of Latino/Chicano and Native American youth and adults through traditional cultural services and facilitate healing, core identity and self-efficacy.
- By increasing exposure to LPI activities, reduce incarceration, recidivism risk and adjudication of Latino/Chicano and Native American youth and adult criminal offenders through innovative, drug-free, income-generating activities that promote entrepreneurship, art and

educational development of high-risk area youth and inmates.

• Increase the organizational capacity of La Plazita to sustain its healing services while retaining its community-based and indigenous healing philosophy.

• Reduce race-based and ethnic disparities of Latino/ Chicano and Native Americans through engagement in critical prevention work and systemic policy efforts collaboratively with local, state and national stakeholders. Such strategies include shrinking the school-to-prison pipeline by developing and implementing culturally appropriate strategies and best practices to reform the juvenile justice system and address key barriers for Chicano/Hispanic and Native youth and families.

Nontraditional Leadership Institute

Many LPI staff are "BTDTs" (Been There, Done Thats) who have been previously incarcerated or are otherwise familiar with life on the street, but they have now chosen a life of service to the community. These staff members act as nontraditional leaders or role models for local youth and families. They provide youth and community members with opportunities to speak publicly and meet other nontraditional leaders within an expansive network of national and international activists and community leaders.

LPI direct service program activities and talking circles, as well as its ceramics classes, silk-screen print trainings, La Plazita Gardens and allied community outreach efforts all strongly emphasize the importance of leadership and social entrepreneurship through personal, academic and professional development. This work fundamentally seeks to advance meaningful civic engagement for social change. LPI staff members are students and lifelong learners, as is every young person or community member who walks through La Plazita's doors. The experience provided at LPI is intentionally transformative, comprehensive, holistic and multifaceted. All of this work is grounded in the core values of La Cultura Cura.

Making a Change (MAC) Programs

Teens Making a Change (TMAC) engages youth and men participants of all ages, ethnicities and backgrounds. This work involves these men and boys in traditional rituals, educational exchanges, workshops, cultural activities and dialogues. TMAC brings young men together for mentorship and provides a safe place for youth to talk and express themselves. Education and entrepreneurship are a strong emphasis throughout TMAC.

The Warrior Circle provides educational programming and traditional healing circles at Atrisco Heritage Academy High School. This work targets and involves promising at-risk LPI youth program participants and rival gang members. Sessions are opened with traditional prayers, blessings for the food (free meals are always provided) and a *plática* (a heart-to-heart talking circle) where youth openly share a recent "low" and "high" in a safe space, celebrate successes and report stressors or challenges that may be impacting them and their families and surrounding communities.

Sisters Making a Change (SMAC) engages women participants of all ages, ethnicities and backgrounds, involving them in traditional rituals, education, workshops, cultural activities and dialogues. SMAC brings together mature and younger women to advance intergenerational exchange and mentorship opportunities, providing a safe place for participating young women to express themselves. Education and entrepreneurship are a strong program emphasis of SMAC.

People Making a Change (PMAC) offers a safe space where interested community members can talk about regional and grassroots neighborhood needs. In this work, institutional leaders and community members come together to engage in dialogue. This work also supports a series of community educational workshops on topics including criminal justice, health, immigration, parenting, positive youth engagement and economic and community development. PMAC meets monthly and is open to all local parents and families, community leaders, government officials and other stakeholders interested in social change efforts and advocacy on behalf of the poor and disenfranchised.

FoodCorps New Mexico

FoodCorps New Mexico is dedicated to equipping LPI service members with the skills, knowledge and experiences required to address the root causes of food injustice. The corps also provides hands-on training and technical assistance in subjects like organics, desert farming, school gardening, traditional foods and community organizing. See the website foodcorps.org/ for more information.

La Plazita employs a full-time FoodCorps service member who coordinates various La Plazita Gardens programs and educational activities. This typically involves collaborative efforts in partnership with the Agri-Cultura Network to (1) distribute la cosecha (fresh produce boxes for local families), (2) provide nutrition education classes to home child-care providers and patients with diabetes (primarily Spanish-speaking women, including mothers) and (3) offer nutrition and gardening education at various local schools. Through Food-Corps LPI has also developed a mentorship program with the University of New Mexico's College Assistance Migrant Program (CAMP) and Atrisco Heritage Academy High School.

School tours, special projects, community events and public service activities are also built into this work.

FoodCorps Host Organizations

The University of New Mexico Community Engagement Center (CEC) nurtures leadership for community capacity building in neighborhoods where the social determinants of inequity result in major health disparities. More than 800 university, community college and high school students have apprenticed with local partners through CEC AmeriCorps programs. Through civic engagement and antiracism training, corps members gain an understanding of the root causes of health disparities.

Farm to Table focuses on training, technical assistance, policy change and market-based strategies. Its goal is to improve food access that benefits low income communities' and children's health by providing linkages between New Mexico farmers, their crops, school food programs and students. The program trains farmers on institutional sales, food safety and other market issues; it also trains educators and practitioners on agriculture, health, nutrition and culinary subjects, and educates the public and policy makers on healthy-food policy issues.

Pathways

The Pathways Program was created through the EleValle Collaborative and sustained with funding and support from the University of New Mexico Health Sciences Center and the W. K. Kellogg Foundation. Pathways is designed to reduce unmet needs, address health inequities and improve the overall well-being of the residents of Bernalillo County. It focuses on positive health outcomes by utilizing community health navigators as care coordinators who connect at-risk residents to resources and follow their progress toward improved health outcomes. Meaningful outcomes for the clients are reached by following a step-by-step approach (Pathways). While individual clients attain improved health, common systems issues are also brought to light, resulting in strengthened service coordination.

The main goal of Pathways' community-based educators, or *promotores*, through EleValle is to teach each client how to navigate these services so that they, in turn, can become community leaders who help their families, friends and neighbors to utilize complex public and private systems, regardless of race, class or immigration status.

EleValle's Pathways navigators work with community members to assess their risks and needs, connect them to resources in the community, chart their progress toward improved health and identify systemic issues that affect their health and well-being. Navigators work with low-income, uninsured adults with multiple unmet needs in the South Valley and within Bernalillo County who may be experiencing

- homelessness
- hunger
- limited access to needed health care
- barriers trying to navigate the system and/or accessing resources as undocumented and/or limited-English-proficient immigrants
- dislocation from existing resources in Bernalillo County as urban off-reservation Native Americans
- any of the above who are parenting young children
- traditional and cultural healing services (Mexican and urban Native)

Woohokihi

La Plazita Institute's Woohokihi Cultural Program reintroduces Native American urban families and incarcerated Native American populations to their cultural traditions and practices. Some of the weekly services provided are Lakota and Nahuatl language services, Inipi ceremonies, talking circles, rites of passage and immersion in a traditional lifeways program. LPI also offers training on traditional farming methods of the Southwest and culturally relevant "Pathways," or navigation services. Traditional Lifeways services include job readiness, training and entrepreneurship through silk-screen printing and traditional crafts like ceramics, beading, quilting and silversmithing.

Curanderismo

La Plazita Institute offers traditional healing services to all of its clients and staff. Its traditional healing program brings together men, women and families who are affirming, reconnecting and remembering the traditional ancestral methods through which people empower their own healing.

Some of the treatments offered include:

- *limpias* (spiritual energy cleansing)
- *sobadas* (Mesoamerican massage)
- *remedios* (home herbal remedies)
- *ventosas* (cupping)
- aromatherapy
- acudetox
- Reiki
- acupuncture

Curandera healing days are the first and third Wednesdays of each month. Walk-ins are accepted, but preference is given to appointments.

Acudetox is a prevention and treatment program for substance abuse, relapse prevention and harm reduction. The acudetox program has an 80 percent success rate in assisting with craving, anxiety and depression. Acudetox is a free service held weekly for youth, adults and community members in need.

La Plazita provides the following free traditional, spiritual and cultural healing services to individuals and community groups:

- community sweat lodges
- Santa Fe prison sweat lodges
- Bernalillo County Metropolitan Detention Center pipe ceremonies
- Bernalillo County Youth Services Center pipe ceremonies
- *Curanderismo* treatments for community by both request and appointment

Social Enterprise: La Plazita Gardens

La Plazita Gardens is a place where ideas, practices and opportunity thrive. At LPG traditional culture, spirituality and horticulture come together to meet social entrepreneurship for improvement of the broader community. LPG is comprised of three farm properties: Sánchez, Chávez and Martínez.

A certified organic farm located in the heart of Albuquerque's South Valley, LPG runs year-round food production, growing a wide range of vegetables and fruits. LPG is a founding member and produces in support of the Agri-Cultura Network, and through this collaborative its food is featured in many restaurants, local grocery stores and elements of the Albuquerque Public Schools cafeteria menus.

LPG provides direct financial support to La Plazita Institute's farm production operations and offers a valuable learning space for the institute's educational programming and social enterprise activities. LPG focuses on poverty reduction, food security, socioeconomic justice and land and water reclamation while providing the opportunity for youth and community members to reconnect to their agricultural heritage.

Silk-screen Printing

La Plazita has a silk-screen printing and design space for community youth to express their talents as artists. Here they develop skills that will launch them into self-sufficiency, and they are exposed to entrepreneurship opportunities that will effectively encourage them in thinking about business, innovation, arts and crafts as viable economic ventures. The primary goal is to make a positive change in the lives of marginalized local youth. LPI provides high-risk youth with healthy and positive alternatives to detention and encourages them to pursue their passion and increase their skills while instilling in them a sense of cultural pride, nonviolence and self-determination. This work supports our local youth and adults in the criminal justice system and in the general community in order to provide learning opportunities and skills development. Such efforts offer these young people a way to speak without speaking, a chance to experience an alternative to the negative and to the meaninglessness of conventional visual space.

Ceramics

Ceramics is a form of art therapy for both children and adults, and all age groups are welcome to partake of this free community resource. The Youth and Girls Reporting Center serves adjudicated youth who participate in ceramics workshops and art projects twice weekly. In addition, LPI provides these youth with postrelease opportunities as well as open weekly community walk-in workshops. In the summer of 2014, LPI started an open and free summer program twice weekly (every Tuesday and Thursday, 10 a.m. to 3 p.m.) through which community members, youth and families participate in free culture, art and healing programming.

Conclusion

Frank de Jesús Acosta and Henry A. J Ramos

The purpose of *Overcoming Disparity* is to contribute to the national dialogue regarding the disparities facing Latino (and Native) boys and men in California and other states of the American Southwest. While the root causes of these young men's precarious condition in American society are fundamentally linked to the ongoing struggle to ameliorate poverty and the lingering specter of racism, there is growing evidence that these impediments to progress can be significantly addressed through the scaling and replication of new models of community-based prevention and intervention, such as those highlighted here. These efforts, in fact, are showing the way to a better path and potentiality for young Latino males.

A national men and boys of color movement has emerged during recent years that holds great promise for helping to bridge the abyss that disparities create for this increasingly important population of Americans. The White House My Brother's Keeper Initiative, spearheaded by President Barack Obama, represents a watershed in this nation's history. Symbolically, it acknowledges to the nation that the full benefits of democracy are being systematically denied to young men of color. The President's call to action has been further amplified during recent months by the righteous indignation of African Americans and others concerned about police policies and practices concerning communities of color in the form of the Black Lives Matter Movement.

Our recent work to document the issues affecting Latino men and boys and to highlight proven organizational models and program interventions that are demonstrating positive results for these youngsters is very much in line with this timely national moment of truth. We seek to contribute to the growing national dialogue about men and boys of color by expanding the evidence base related to prevention and intervention models that demonstrate real impact in Latino community settings. By positively engaging Latino men and boys and creating more robust opportunities for them to grow, learn and contribute their many inherent talents to the solution of our nation's and the world's ever-increasing challenges, these models, scaled and replicated, portend better things to come for our nation as a whole.

The alternative of staying the course we have been on seems to us and most informed observers to be a self-defeating proposition. Presently, America spends nearly $75 billion annually to warehouse our adult prison population. Our Latino populations across the country are fast growing and consist increasingly of young people and first- or second-generation immigrants. By the midpoint of the current century, demographic experts estimate, more than one-quarter of our national population will be of Latino origin. Our very future as a functioning democracy and global economic leader hangs in the balance if we cannot find a way to better harness the presently underutilized and underresourced capacities of this population—and especially the millions of young men and boys who are a significant part of it.

At the outset of the twentieth century, a hundred years ago, American leaders faced similar circumstances as large populations of immigrants from Ireland, Italy and various Eastern European nations disembarked at Ellis Island. The immigrants of the American past came in search of democratic and economic opportunities unavailable to them in their countries of origin. In response, US policy makers and civic leaders made strategic decisions to invest in the building of new infra-structures, institutions and programs that set the stage for effective immigrant integration across our society. They invested in public libraries and schools to educate and inform the immigrant newcomers in the ways of American culture. They prioritized the building of bridges, dams and highways that fueled a generation of robust national economic growth. And through private philanthropy, they supported the cre-ation of self-help settlement houses, community service organizations and civic networks whose work provided succor and support to America's huddled masses.

These developments, in turn, enabled our nation to unify in ways that otherwise would not have been likely. As a result, America was able to prevail and ultimately come out ahead through the tribulations of the Great Depression, World War II and the Cold War. Today, notwithstanding the denial of many present-day American policy leaders, our circumstances require an equally sweeping national investment to integrate our still effectively disenfranchised communities of color and immi-grants. Particularly important in this connection is the urgent need to invest in the future success of men and boys of color, whose challenges are on the rise on multiple fronts: from very high education incompletion and incarceration rates to depressed wage-earning capacities and a significant incidence of poverty. Our focus in this publication and in a companion book that was recently released is on the particular circum-stances and opportunities facing Latino men and boys and the emergence of winning response models that warrant expanded institutional recognition and support. The first of the two books we have produced on the issues, *Latino Young Men and Boys in Search of Justice: Testimonies*, will, we hope, fuel a sense of heightened urgency and imperative to respond more fully and honestly to the needs of Latino men and boys. The book lifts up the authentic voices of these young men through the showcasing of their original art, poetry and heartfelt writings. The featured essays represent a glimpse into the hard realities faced by young people who have experienced and overcome disparity themselves, many of whom have since dedicated their lives to working for progressive change in their communities. They also lift up the voices and wisdom of seasoned practitioners, activist artists, writers, grassroots field leaders and others, who reflect on the inherent healing and transformative power of the arts and culture to elevate humanity.

These intergenerational voices offer profound insights into the comprehensive efforts taking place across California and the nation to address the issues. The present volume, the second book in our series, has offered up profiles in best practice, featuring two of the nation's leading culturally proficient program, organizational and community-wide models for dismantling disparity and improving the quality of life for Latino and other men and boys of color: the National Compadres Network, based in Southern California, and La Plazita Institute, based in northern New Mexico.

The commanding voices and organizations featured in both publications are leading champions of best practice in restorative justice, education equity, healthy human development, community transformation and civic engagement. They call their movement La Cultura Cura (The Healing Culture). In addition to the National Compadres Network and La Plazita Institute, which are profiled in this book, other leading model organizations and programs in the field include Santa Cruz Barrios Unidos, Communities United for Restorative Youth Justice, Homies Unidos and Homeboy Industries. Our book series recognizes the birthrights of inheritance that many Latinos deserve from having deep ancestral ties to this continent that predate the establishment of the United States. In conjunction with these publications, we have constructed a shared webpage featuring supplemental best practice profiles at artepublicopress.com and on the Insight Center for Community Economic Development's corporate website, insightcced.org.

As highlighted throughout our NCN and LPI profiles herein, the fundamental unifying core element of all of the best practice models we cover is that their guiding values, principles and strategies are rooted in and/or significantly informed by the philosophy of La Cultura Cura. It is our informed opinion, as well as that of our expert panel of advisors, that cultural fluency and proficiency must be the cornerstones of any discipline or model that can be legitimately designated as a best practice in the healing, transformation and nurturing of Latino men and boys. In this regard, the La Cultura Cura philosophy and framework embody the essential tenets of best practice across disciplines, programs and systems.

During recent years, some of the nation's most cutting-edge efforts in the men and boys of color movement have been supported by visionary philanthropic organizations. These include the major funders who supported the development of this publication series: the California Endowment, W. K. Kellogg Foundation, Sierra Health Foundation, Marguerite Casey Foundation and the California Community Foundation. Organizations like these have been at the forefront of needed change in this space. Readers may wish to investigate some of the notable public-private partnerships and philanthropic efforts funders like these have supported with an eye to engaging policy change, systems change, applied research and practice innovations related to men and boys of color:

• Alameda County Coalition for Criminal Justice Reform
• the California Endowment's Building Healthy Communities initiative

- Dignity in Schools Campaign
- Fresno Boys and Men of Color
- Gathering for Justice
- Hispanics in Philanthropy Southwest Latino Men and Boys Initiative
- W. K. Kellogg Foundation's investments in boys and young men of color
- PolicyLink's Alliance for Boys and Men of Color
- The White House My Brother's Keeper Initiative
- Sierra Health Foundation's Positive Youth Justice Initiative
- Urban Strategies Council's Boys and Men of Color initiative

Presently, and happily, there appears to be an encouraging increase in catalytic philanthropic investment toward growing the field. In 2015, for example, the leaders of twenty-six of the nation's leading philanthropic organizations met in Chicago to advance a collective campaign to address issues facing men and boys of color in US civic engagement, education, employment, economic development, health, media and the arts. The gathering was held concurrently with the annual meeting of the Council on Foundations. The foundations wishing to make public their engagement in this field-building effort include:

- Annie E. Casey Foundation
- the Boston Foundation
- California Community Foundation
- the California Endowment
- Casey Family Programs
- Community Foundation of South Alabama
- Denver Foundation
- Foundation for the Mid South
- Headwaters Foundation for Justice

- John S. and James L. Knight Foundation
- the Kresge Foundation
- Liberty Hill Foundation
- Living Cities
- Lumina Foundation
- Marguerite Casey Foundation
- Mary Reynolds Babcock Foundation
- Mitchell Kapor Foundation
- Open Society Foundations
- Robert Wood Johnson Foundation
- Schott Foundation for Public Education
- Sierra Health Foundation
- Silicon Valley Community Foundation
- Skillman Foundation
- Tides Foundation
- W. K. Kellogg Foundation
- Winthrop Rockefeller Foundation

As we suggested at the beginning of this narrative, given present demographic trends in the United States, our social and economic viability and competitiveness as a nation increasingly depend on new investments and explorations intended to enhance the health and well-being of Latino men and boys and their families. Prolonged disparity, overt injustice and de facto sanctioned discrimination can only breed desperation, growing frustration and alienation in our society. Disregarding or suppressing the Latino people and their cultures is self-defeating for the nation. We propose a better and smarter path: namely, a major national reinvestment in the principles of pluralism and democratic practice that can help to ensure this important population's success in ways that ultimately serve the interests of all Americans.

We think the time has come for us to collectively examine the soul of our nation and to assess more honestly the state of our democracy. The Declaration of Independence states, "We hold these truths to be self-evident, that all men are created equal, that they are endowed by their Creator with certain unalienable Rights, and that among these are Life, Liberty and the pursuit of Happiness." It is hard to square these words and commitments with the present-day legal, social, cultural, economic and political status and treatment of our nation's large and growing population of Latino men and boys and their families.

Our first book, *The History of Barrios Unidos: Healing Community Violence*, states, "Each generation's struggle for justice is framed against the backdrop of chronic inequality. Thus, perhaps, the most accurate bell-weather for the vitality of American democracy today is the welfare of our children and the degree to which poverty and violence permeate the fabric of our society." We submit this book, and the series of which it is a part, in good faith as our contribution to the emerging national dialogue on Latino and other men and boys of color. We conclude with a quote from one of the leading elders of the community peace movement, Daniel "Nane" Alejandrez, from his speech to close Santa Cruz Barrios Unidos' twenty-fifth anniversary celebration:

> We are at a cultural and spiritual crossroads where we must reclaim the truth and traditions of our heritage as we move forward towards the promise of our future. As we have learned to know and respect ourselves, we have learned to honor and respect the dignity of others. We need to practice nonviolence and embrace old and new partnerships with those that share our vision for equal social and economic justice for all people. This is the true and only path to peace and the mutual well-being of all.

Appendix

Maestro Jerry Tello at intercultural gathering.

Gathering of Wisdom: a cohosted intergenerational, inter-group dialogue.

Sundance chief Albino García, Jr., at circle ceremony.

La Plazita Institute participants in prayer.

OUR YOUTH

... Are Sacred

... Have a Sacred Purpose

... Have teachers from within their culture

... Carry ancestral wisdom

... Deserve a safe place to allow them to Learn, Heal, Grow, and Lead.

HEALING GENERATIONS

www.nationalcompadresnetwork.com

Promotional poster for National Compadres Network.

Healing Generations chart.

Statement from Frank de Jesús Acosta

We are a continuation of our ancestors, their struggles and their journeys for collective and personal dignity. My art expresses the vitality, strength, and tenacity of indigenous people, those who share the vision of a healthy Mother Earth. With art I offer visual affirmations of our inherent spiritual existence. With art I offer visual remedies from attempted termination, war, displacement and resulting trauma.